The Crime Against Europe

A Possible Outcome of the War of 1914

By Roger Casement

With an introductory essay by
Angus Mitchell

Introduction © Angus Mitchell

Published by The dlr Roger Casement Summer School

Printed and bound by GPS, 4 Marshalls Road, Belfast, BT56SR, Northern Ireland

Origination and design by Conleth Adamson,
ICON Graphic Services, 73 Foxfield Grove, Raheny, Dublin, D05 TX32, Ireland.

ISBN: 978-1-9997297-0-7

CONTENTS

Preface

The dlr 1916 Committee published a book on Dún Laoghaire Rathdown and 1916 and a series of lectures on many of its leading figures, including Roger Casement, who was born on Lawson Terrace in Dún Laoghaire on 1 September 1864. The DLRCC agreed to remember Casement by commissioning a statue, and agreeing to support a dlr Roger Casement Summer School, proposed by the dlr 1916 Committee. As a supplement to this event, it was agreed to republish Casement's *The Crime Against Europe*, with an introduction by the historian and cultural critic, Angus Mitchell. The support of the DLRCC and the New Ireland Assurance Company has been crucial in the completion of this endeavour and we would like to thank them for their support.

The Crime Against Europe is a collection of articles written by Casement in the period before the outbreak of the 1914-18 war. A conflict fought mainly among Europe's imperial powers. Casement argued that if any such war came about, it would be a crime against the people of Europe. He pointed the finger of blame at the elite ruling class in England as primarily responsible for fostering hatred. And so it proved to be, an estimated 17 million killed and 20 million injured.

Casement was a strong advocate of Irish neutrality, which he hoped would be intrinsic to the foreign policy of any future independent state. In these essays, he makes the argument that supports the triangulated dream of Irish sovereign independence rooted in a European Ireland defending a policy of neutrality. He envisioned a Congress of Europe, a congress of sovereign states, and, above all, a Europe at peace . His views and actions would ultimately cost him his life.

So despite the fact that these essays were first published over 100 years ago they have a clear relevance today. Brexit, the debate on the future of the European Union, the spectre of the border, the enduring tensions with Russia, and unending global conflicts in the Middle East, all lend Casement's analysis a contemporary relevance.

Roger Cole Chair dlr Roger Casement Summer School 2017

'It is only the truth that wounds': Revisiting Roger Casement's *The Crime Against Europe*

In 1921, as the focus on the War of Independence in Ireland shifted towards the negotiating table, an official British parliamentary report was published in London containing evidence about the active connections between leaders of the Easter Rising and Germany.[1] This compilation of documents opened with scrutiny of the writings of Roger Casement and his authorship of diverse essays published between 1911 to the outbreak of the war in 1914. The earliest collection of Casement's articles happened within weeks of the outbreak of conflict.[2] Over the next two years, as the European war became a world war, large runs of this pamphlet were printed in America and Germany. It was given the title *The Crime against Europe*. French and German translations were also published.[3]

Scrutiny of the impact of this small book lies beyond the scope of this introduction. Some copies were smuggled across borders and made their way to Ireland, where they were distributed clandestinely. In essence, the nine short essays consolidated Casement's analysis of why any eventual conflict between the British Empire and Germany was not Ireland's war. What is both significant and remarkable about these essays is that they were almost all scripted well in advance of the war. Three of the essays were written in March 1913, as Casement made his last journey to Africa to visit his brother Tom at his farm in the Drakensburg Mountains. There he hoped to spend a few weeks recovering from his exhaustive investigation of the mistreatment of the indigenous communities living in the north-west Amazon. Another three essays were written at the end of that year, as Casement committed himself fully to the founding of the Irish Volunteers and undertook a series of recruitment rallies across Ireland.

Casement believed that the publication of these articles would one day vindicate his actions and illuminate the path that would ultimately lead him to the scaffold. In the weeks before his execution, he scribbled instructions after the war for the publication of his political writings.[4] In a letter dated a few days before his execution, he wrote 'Remember that it is *The Crime Against Europe* that is the key to all recent doings in

Ireland.'[5] But this claim is still highly controversial and in various ways cuts against the grain of much of the historiography of recent times that persists in validating the sacrifice of Irish soldiers in the defence of the British Empire. Casement has not been allowed to pass so easily into history. These essays and his corpus of political writings require the reader to reassess the causes of the First World War in ways that profoundly challenge dominant narratives. As one recent commentator has put it: 'if thinking is done on the basis of what Casement wrote then the whole narrative of the Great War collapses.'[6]

In the wake of a century of analytical history about the First World War, the failure to publish an edition of Casement's writings in line with his final wishes, says much about the troubled status of Casement within both British and Irish historiography. Though Casement was a prominent intellectual of his age and he emerged in 2016 at the centre of commemorative politics, there remains an anxiety about knowing too much about the man or, indeed, critiquing his evaluation of why the world was propelled into war. Margaret O'Callaghan has observed how 'Casement's analysis of high political intrigue was often well-informed and based on a personal knowledge of many of the key political actors.'[7] Was it this insight of the inner workings of power that made his revelations so potentially rupturing to his contemporaries and still so challenging to current orthodoxies?

All his essays are punctuated with a deep reading of Irish history tempered by a thoughtful grasp of both the structure and process of the past. At once his reflections on his time are wry, witty, angry and emotive. Casement's analysis can be both crushingly candid and unsettling in the prescient honesty of how he interprets world events. His commentary on another level draws to a conclusion the much deeper investigation of empire and colonial power relations that informed his official career. There are moments when his emersion in his investigation of the tragedy of the pre-Columbian world of South America collides with his deepening criticism of the colonial relationship between England and Ireland.

Borrowing from his reading of the Amazon naturalist Henry Bates, he compared the British Empire to a tropical liana, the *Sipo Matador* – a murdering creeper, or parasitic plant that attaches itself to large trees and then stealthily spreads over the trunk, like a 'plastic mould', feeding off the vitality of the tree until it has sapped all its strength. At another point, and this time borrowing from the observations noted by the natural scientist Charles Darwin, when off the coast of Bahia during his voyage on *HMS Beagle*, Casement compared Ireland to the Diodon. This small fish if swallowed whole by a shark could eat its way out of the intestines of its predator, devouring its way through the stomach walls and skin until it had escaped from the body. In this path to freedom, the shark dies. Casement felt this would ultimately define Ireland's relationship to the British Empire.

Considered in their entirety, the essays provide a unique and often highly critical insight into British foreign policy and the causes of war. Casement argued unequivocally that the war was largely a consequence of a deliberate strategy to alienate Germany and subvert its economic advancement and competitiveness. He argued too that the independence of Ireland would prove to be an essential requisite to a peaceful future in Europe and a convincing case is made for a European Ireland.

During Casement's long involvement with the British Foreign Office he had witnessed Britain's relations deteriorate with Germany in a way that might have been avoided had the mentality of the British imperial mind been different. Anxiety is apparent in all of these essays that war in Europe is inevitable. When that war came about, Casement's admonition seemed both prescient and logical, but the arguments endured as profoundly upsetting to the official narrative of events. As Casement commented at the outset of this collection: 'To find the causes of the war we should turn not to Blue Books or White Papers, giving carefully selected statements of those responsible for concealing from the public the true issues that move nations to attack each other, but should seek the unavowed aims of those nations themselves.' His essays examined many such unavowed aims.

Their identification by 1921 as a key instrument of 'propaganda' in the Irish independence movement says much about their impact in the eyes of the British government. We should be in little doubt that the intelligence services, tasked with capturing this renegade knight of the realm and engineering his humiliating end on the scaffold in central London, were well aware of these writings and the threat they posed to official versions of 'truth'.

In England, the circumstance surrounding Casement's tragic and toxic execution did little to encourage public interest in his intellectual intervention in the Irish struggle. There was little need for the public to know too much about this renegade consul. But feelings within Irish nationalist circles were very different. Casement's stature within the revolutionary underground remained on a level with both James Connolly and Patrick Pearse. But after the signing of the Anglo-Irish treaty in 1921 and the establishment of the Irish Free State, interest in Casement was driven to the margins. His relevance to the conflict of 1914-18 and his role in Ireland's fight for freedom were gradually isolated. *The Crime against Europe* was cast into the recesses of historical consciousness and Casement's voice of reason was denied oxygen.

In 1958, Herbert Mackey, a Dublin-based skin doctor devoted to retrieving Casement's name into the nationalist canon and vindicating his name, published the first Irish edition of *The Crime against Europe*.[8] By then enough time had passed to allow both historians and commentators to recognise that much of what Casement argued was neither particularly radical nor treasonous. In fact, his commentary and critique could now be read for its measured prescience. For those who considered the sacrifices of the First World War as an unfathomable crime against humanity, his objections were both lucid and reasonable.

The articles collected together in *The Crime against Europe* knit together various arguments of both a moderate and a more radical and progressive nature. The most trenchant element of the argument makes the case as to why Ireland's sympathies should lie with Germany and not with Britain. Casement considered the war quite literally to be a crime against Europe, perpetrated by a ruling elite in Britain prepared to sacrifice millions of lives in order to maintain Britain's imperial advantage. He argued that the duty of the Irish people struggling for some level of national sovereignty should be to support Germany in that conflict. The introduction made the point clear: 'the vital needs of European peace, of European freedom of the seas and of Irish national life and prosperity were indissolubly linked with the cause of Germany.' In other essays, notably *Ireland, Germany and the Next War* and *The Elsewhere Empire*, he made the case that if Ireland had a grievance with any of the protagonists involved, then it was with England and the British Empire: the agents of Ireland's economic and cultural servitude.

Casement's argument for an Irish alliance with Germany was a position that had developed out of his own experience and analysis of European relations in the decade leading up to conflict. During those years, he had criticised the rising tempo of anti-German sentiment promoted by the British press and in the culture of secret diplomacy within the corridors of Whitehall. In a letter written to his colleague in the Congo Reform Association, ED Morel, sent whilst serving as British consul general in Rio de Janeiro in 1909, he had quite candidly predicted the coming conflict:

> The Entente Cordiale is at the bottom of it all, but it is because in quite another sense Germany is at the bottom. Instead of trying to arrive at a generally friendly arrangement with Germany on all points, which would obviously include the Congo, we have gone out of our way for several years now to eliminate Germany from our councils and as far as we could from the councils of others. We have tried to bottle up very new wine indeed in very old diplomatic bottles and the bursting will cut many hands and perhaps an artery. Now things have reached so evil a pass

that peace between the two great powers of Europe can hardly be kept. Both are preparing for war and faster than the world at large suspects – but the fault lies far more with England than with Germany. It has been a wretchedly stupid business – based first on jealousy, trade, ill will and greed of commerce and now resting largely on fear too. The English have become afraid of the Germans, afraid of German expansion, of German commercial training, of the German fleet even – and so the entente with France has become more and more a necessity to her statesmanship. I said years ago the power to make the Entente with was Germany – that I should have invited Germany into Morocco or anywhere else she wanted to go – to Brazil for one – where her expansion would not hurt the British Empire. Now the miserable effort at bottling up Germany has gone so far it is hard to get back to sober statesmanship.[9]

Casement's opposition to the war was rooted firmly in a reading of just war theory. In both his published and private writings, he disputed the legitimacy of Britain to make war (*jus ad bellum*) and condemned British, French and Russian antagonism towards Germany as constituted not upon common interests or aims, but rather upon mutual aggression.[10] His view was simple: Ireland and the Irish people had no quarrel with Germany and therefore they should refuse to enlist in a fight in defence of their oppressors. The essays make the case that the war was both unnecessary and illegal. In that sense his arguments have cut acutely against the grain of how the war has been both processed and structured within the public imagination as a 'just war': or a war in defence of freedom; a war to unite us all; or, most absurdly, a war to end all wars.

Once war was declared, Casement took the decision to turn his back on the British Empire that had honoured him during twenty years of apparently loyal service. With the approval and financial support of the executive council of Clan na Gael in New York, he became an ambassador for the Irish independence movement. In October 1914, he left America and made his way to Berlin to open negotiations with the German Foreign Office.[11] He would remain in Germany for the next eighteen months.

Initially, he tried to raise an Irish Brigade and to extract guarantees from the German Foreign Office that the interests of Ireland would be safeguarded in the event of a German victory. But as his recruitment efforts met with failure and indifference, and as the war was locked into a bloody stalemate on the Western Front, Casement's disillusionment deepened. His attentions shifted instead to turning the barrel of his pen against the Whitehall establishment that had honoured him. He started to publish regularly in an English-language newspaper published in Berlin, *The Continental*

Times. In a stream of essays published in the latter half of 1915, he revealed some dark official secrets of British imperial power, which did little to endear him to his former paymasters. His anger was levelled too at the escalating deployment of the press to subvert public understanding of events. His preoccupations turned now to the conduct of war (*jus in bello*) and the calculated abuse of truth in order to sustain and widen the conflict. This commentary on the vicious perpetuation of falsehoods reached beyond defiance into a realm of unanswerable conspiracy.[12]

After his return to Ireland aboard a German submarine in April 1916, he was captured shortly after his landing at Banna Strand and then spirited out of the country. His last view of Ireland was here in Dún Laoghaire (Kingstown) where he boarded a passenger ferry on the evening of Easter Saturday 1916 under police escort. He had come full circle. It was a mile or so from there in Lawson Terrace on Sandyford Road where he was born on 1 September 1864. So it is quite appropriate that Dún Laoghaire should take ownership of Roger Casement through an annual summer school and a monument dedicated to his achievements and his memory. Both the beginning and end of Casement's life in Ireland are intimately connected with this district of Dublin.

Casement's trial for high treason happened at the height of the First World War. The trial was a remarkably bitter affair. Casement's sworn enemy, the leading Unionist MP, cabinet minister and the Attorney General, FE Smith, led the prosecution. With him stood several of the most able and pitiless judicial minds in the land. With the war at a critical juncture, the trial was unavoidably political. The judge appointed to preside was Rufus Isaacs, who would later become Viceroy of India, where he demonstrated a chilling detachment in his treatment of the Indian national liberator, Mahatma Gandhi. The full force of British law was deployed to deliver a verdict of guilty. The sentence of death by hanging was pronounced at the end of June 1916, just forty-eight hours before the opening explosion at the Battle of the Somme. But Casement's speech from the dock would resonate down the ages.[13]

In the weeks that followed the trial, various petitions and personal appeals to the government demanding clemency proved unsuccessful. A number of those appeals were forthcoming from the citizenry of Dún Laoghaire. But the protests fell on deaf ears. Even though his closest friends and relatives maintained pressure on an intransigent government, Casement was reconciled to his end. His prison writings reveal a serene acceptance of the verdict. It is now clear that since his youth, he had identified with the long roll call of Ireland's martyred dead. History, he believed, would one day vindicate his actions and the logic of his treason would be explained.

But the authorities had other plans. The trial had initiated a vicious process of dehumanisation and humiliation of a reviled traitor. A smear campaign was set in motion that in many respects reflected the depth of abhorrence felt by those in authority in Britain for what Casement had done and all he stood for.[14] His treason pierced the armour of British power in ways that could not and would not be forgiven. The logic of his anti-imperialism could neither be tolerated nor understood. Elaborate efforts were set in motion to confuse Casement's heroic work exposing the dark heart of empire.

His case was further complicated because his name was associated more than any other executed leader of the Easter Rising with the province of Ulster. Many of Casement's closest friends were part of a network of cultural nationalists associated closely with Ulster's cultural revival. That coterie included notable poets such as Alice Milligan, Cathal O'Byrne and Joseph Campbell, the artist Ada McNeill, the antiquarian Francis Joseph Bigger, the scholar revolutionary Eoin MacNeill, the Rosicrucian mystic Rose Young, and various language scholars such as Margaret Dobbs. If the authorities had found it hard to control Casement's accusatory voice during his life, they found it equally difficult to control him in death.

In the ensuing years, every effort was made to suggest that Casement's bold deed of open treason was the result of a 'deluded', 'mad', 'egotistical' or 'excessively emotional' individual. After his lime bleached bones were disinterred and returned to Ireland in 1965, a steady stream of memoirs and biographies sought to carefully manage his narrative in ways that supported his merciless treatment. Critical parts of his archive were destroyed.[15] The logic of his evolution into an enemy of empire was scrambled in the public imagination. But because the Casement secret was itself masterminded by those with a commanding knowledge of history, the eventual unlocking of that secret still proves to be a particularly Byzantine affair.

Mapping Casement's evolution from loyal servant of the crown into incorrigible traitor was perceived as utterly loathsome to the ruling imperial establishment in Britain. In 1911, following his knighthood in the Coronation honours list of King George V, he was endorsed as the moral conscience of the British Empire. Newspapers across the world acclaimed him as a man of outstanding integrity. His investigations of what we recognise today as human rights abuses in sub-Saharan Africa and South America awakened both governments and the public to the destructive capacity of unregulated market forces and the nefarious side effects of capitalism.

That analysis of the systemic colonial violence underlying the civilising process of Belgium's King Leopold II's activities in the Congo combined with his exposure of the role of British investment capital in the destruction of rainforest communities and environment in the northwest Amazon shook the foundations of European civilisation. Yet, a century on, Casement's criticism of empire was no different from the position taken today on trade by organisations such as Survival International, Antislavery International or various anti-war movements. But once evaluated in the context of his self-proclaimed treason and with the security and reputation of the British Empire threatened by his revelations, his views could not be tolerated.

But if those views and acts would be condemned by the reactionary structures of power in Britain, Casement's achievement found respect and admiration elsewhere. Among an emerging group of activists, pacifists, socialists and internationalists, his critique of the affairs of empire proved inspiring to subject peoples and oppressed communities searching for justice and rights around the world. Over the next century, his life, death and legacy would endure as a symbol for anti-colonial struggle in many different corners of the world. Among those who drew strength and meaning from his life and actions might be counted the Marxist revolutionary Rosa Luxemburg, the Pan-African leader, Kwame Nkrumah and independent India's first prime minister, Jawaharlal Nehru.

During the centenary commemorations last year, a number of leading contemporary critics with deep connections to Ireland paid homage to Casement. They included the journalists Patrick Cockburn, Martina Devlin and Robert Fisk and the director of Antislavery International, Aidan McQuade.[16] In 2017, during his state visit to South America, President Michael D. Higgins made a resounding defence of Casement in the Peruvian Ministry of Foreign Affairs. His speech explored the contemporary relevance of Casement in the context of 'globalization': the collective responsibility to mitigate environmental destruction and the deepening tensions born of social injustice:

> If Roger Casement's voice continues to call out to us, it is probably in part because the times he lived through were ones that have profound resonance with our own. Often referred to as the "first globalisation", it was an era when an insatiable capital moved freely across the globe, when vast territorial expanses were opened up to industrial exploitation, with devastating impact on what had been complex civilisations, and when the flow of goods circulating within and between Europe's huge colonial empires increased dramatically. It was a time, too, of great migration, which saw tens of millions of Europeans leave the old continent to seek their fortunes in other hemispheres.
>
> The turn of the twentieth century was also marked by Europe's rapid industrial boom and a race for extractive rubber resources that resulted in

the violent transformation of extensive swathes of latex-bearing tropical forest in the interior regions of Africa and Latin America. This was most intensely felt by the indigenous people living along the basins of the two largest rivers feeding into the Atlantic: The Congo and the Amazon. Indeed, the globalised networks of European commercial expansionism, and the associated process of internal colonisation in the new South American Republics, were predicated upon a system of enslavement and exploitation of the local populations, of which the so-called "Congo Free State" and the frontier region of the north-west Amazon, were two hubs.

Roger Casement was a witness to the crimes perpetrated in both regions. But he was never a passive witness. He did not avert his gaze from those atrocities committed in the pursuit of profit and greed, yet rationalised in the name of progress and civilisation. And it is important, today, that we recall the detail of those sombre aisles of global history, a history in which we all share.[17]

The essays collected in *The Crime Against Europe* offer an alternative insight into the causes of the First World War observed by a government insider with privileged access to the inner workings of political and diplomatic power. It is worth restating that all the essays were written between the summer of 1911 and the end of 1913, apart from the opening chapter, penned in the summer of 1914, on *The Causes of the War and the Foundations of the Peace*. This was the period when Casement's own misgivings about the empire hardened. His exposure to the Amazon frontier stimulated his concerns about the relationship between the imperial centre and the colonised periphery. But the context of these essays belongs too to the long saga over Irish home rule and the deepening crisis within Liberal Party circles. It is important, too, not to loose sight of the political volatility of world affairs in the years before the war: militant suffrage, syndicalism and anarchism were all in different ways flourishing.

Wide-ranging and often acutely unsettling, Casement blended his knowledge of contemporary politics with a frank interpretation of the centuries of conflict between British power and Irish resistance. His command of history was woven judiciously into a measured reading of the world crisis from the perspective of a compassionate humanist: one who despised war and the culture of violence. Although Casement is popularly misremembered as a "gun-runner", his life was a long protest against violence – a position condensed in that stark admission on the eve of his execution: 'My dominating thought was to keep Ireland out of the war. England has no claim on us, in Law or Morality or Right. Ireland should not sell her soul for any mess of Empire.'

Casement's own privileged access to power enabled him to challenge official representations of the war. He condemned the deliberate deepening of antagonism towards Germany and the undeclared elements that had propelled Europe to this point. His essays ask profound questions about imperial governance. What were the deeper motives of the combatants? Was the impending crisis the inevitable outcome of an escalating culture of secret diplomacy? Whose interests would ultimately be best served by war? How was the official narrative of events controlled by the deployment of propaganda techniques? But in asking such questions about imperial governance and its consequences, Casement was not a voice in the wilderness. The advanced nationalist press of this time is filled with news and opinions about the overreach of empire. Conscientious objectors from across Europe were rallying against social injustice, rising inequality and politically unaccountable governance. Casement was intrinsic to that wider chorus.

His main collaborator in the Congo Reform Association, E.D. Morel underwent a parallel transition between 1911 and 1914.[18] In the aftermath of the Agadir Crisis of 1911, Morel published *Morocco in Diplomacy* opening his campaign into the mechanism of secret diplomacy that had brought Europe to the edge of the abyss. On the outbreak of war, Morel stepped into the breech as one of the founders of the Union of Democratic Control. His energies moved from Congo reform towards organising protest against the war and building a conversation and alliance towards peace. The UDC attracted a powerful group of politicians and public intellectuals in opposition to the war. This coterie included the future and first Labour Party Prime Minister, Ramsay MacDonald, the philosopher and mathematician, Bertrand Russell, and the historian and aesthete Vernon Lee. Several ideas and themes developed in *The Crime against Europe* have clear echoes in Morel's own shifting perspective. Equally, there are palpable resonances in the anti-war writings of the German socialist, Karl Liebknecht and other political commentators on the Left.

The earliest essay in *The Crime Against Europe*, appearing under the title *The Keeper of the Seas*, was written in August 1911, a summer of co-ordinated industrial action in Britain. Casement had returned from his voyage of investigation into the upper Amazon at the start of the year and he would return to that region in mid-August. During his nine months back in Europe, he moved between London and Ireland witnessing and analysing the social disintegration and fearful of the escalating political unrest.[19] He grew more impatient of the engrained Germanophobic views held by his colleagues in the Foreign Office reinforced by the popular antagonism disseminated through the organs of mass circulation newspapers. He argued that in any realignment of power relations in Europe, Ireland was the crucial factor. If Ireland could be freed from its economic and cultural servitude to the empire then it would naturally recalibrate European relations for the better. In making his case, Casement invoked both the plight of the Mexican peasantry and the spectre of the Irish famine as components of the same abusive political economy. Over many centuries, Ireland had been held in a bond of peonage and servitude to the empire from which it must now break free.

In his essay, *The Balance of Power*, written in September 1912, as the Home Rule Bill passed through the House of Commons and Unionists in Ulster lined up behind Sir Edward Carson to sign the Solemn League and Covenant, Casement developed further the theme of Ireland's need to integrate with European and Atlantic economies rather than remain the recruiting vassal and economic minion of Britain's empire. This time his argument was situated more directly in a long historical continuum. He considered the dependence of the British empire on Ireland for its strategic imperial advantage and how the empire would not survive if Ireland was lost. He compared the struggle between the British Empire and Germany as comparable to the wars between Rome and Carthage. German success would ultimately rest on how Ireland emerged from any peace negotiations. If independence could be achieved and properly guaranteed then Ireland would develop as a great commercial asset for both Europe and the wider Atlantic region.

In March, as news of the Curragh "mutiny" escalated tensions, Casement wrote *The Enemy of Peace*. Here he examined how English policy had always been inimical to European peace. Britain sustained her political advantage through geographical separation from the Continent of Europe and a policy of divide and rule. Casement's criticism of covert strategies of imperial defence became more accusatory. A reference was made in this essay to a singular weapon in the armoury of imperial control: the deliberate falsification of history. He had long held an interest in how history had been managed, manufactured, and forged at the will of the powerful and for their protection. If this accusation was only lightly touched on in this essay, it was a theme he would return to in much greater detail in his writings after war had been declared.[20]

He denounced too the arms race of the early twentieth century as 'responsible for the enormous growth of armaments that now overshadows continental civilization.' An outcome, he argued, of British policy and 'its claim to universal right of pre-emption to every zone and region washed by the waves and useful or necessary to the expansion of the white races.' His association of the arms industry to race politics was an argument that is easier to make today when such links are well known. Casement's reading of the colonial frontier provided him with further evidence of the racial divisions of empire. From his years as consul in Brazil, he grew to challenge the Anglo-Saxon alliance supporting imperial interests in London and the U.S. and was stridently critical of the Monroe Doctrine 'palladium of the Anglo-Saxon World Empire'.

In another essay – *The Problem of the Near West* – written in March 1913, Casement compared the Balkan crisis and the break up of the Ottoman Empire to the historical claims of England over Ireland. His scrutiny was highly critical of the duplicitous reasoning behind the moral argument underpinning Britain's deepening antagonism towards Turkey: 'what rights has England to Ireland, to Dublin, to Cork? She holds Ireland by exactly the same title as that by which Turkey has hitherto held Macedonia, Thrace, Salonica – a right of invasion, of seizure, of demoralization.' This argument again reiterated the importance of breaking Britain's naval supremacy and 'sea ownership' as vital requirements for the emergence of a new configuration of European civilization.

In *The Duty of Christendom*, written towards the end of 1913, as Casement's commitment to the Irish Volunteer movement emerged into the open, Casement considered some of the cultural differences between England and Ireland. Once again he endorsed the need for Ireland to consider Germany as their natural ally in the struggle for independence. But the language was increasingly inflammatory: 'how to give our lives for Ireland – that has been, that is the problem of Irish nationality.' The tempo of his criticism of the British Empire was increasingly abrasive. In *The Freedom of the Seas*, he made explicit attacks on the framework of violence sustaining imperial power. This was part of a much deeper analysis of the structural formation of empires. Casement's official life had ultimately turned on his investigation and public denouncements of the excesses of international power. During his twenty years in Africa, he had participated actively in the European territorial 'scramble' and emerged as a very able critic of the relationship between coloniser and the colonised. But as his experience of European empires broadened, and as he personally bore witness to the class, race and gender based violence underpinning imperial relations, he revised his own readings of Ireland's deeper relationship with Britain. As an official, he had witnessed how the vulnerable communities of the Amazon and their ecologies were exposed to the violent cycles of free-market venture capital. [21] His efforts to work from within to bring about reform failed and left him few options but to turn wholly on the system itself.

Casement's analysis contains disturbing revelations about the conduct of British policy in Ireland and within the broader field of international relations that brought about the tragedy of the First World War. What is striking is how some of his damning assessments about the causes of the war are echoed in more contemporary readings. For instance, Niall Ferguson's provocative 1999 interpretation *The Pity of War* challenged the orthodox views on the causes of conflict. He disputed the 'Fischer thesis' that blamed domestic German politics and the Kaiser's expansionist foreign policy for escalating tensions. Ferguson, a political conservative and firm defender of Britain's imperial past, condemned the First World War as a disastrous conflict of mainly England's making, and provoked by incompetent diplomacy led by the British Foreign Secretary, Sir Edward Grey. Such an argument in different ways tallies with several strands of Casement's views, although Ferguson omits the faintest acknowledgment of any such connection to that source. Conversely, the critique of various Marxist historians arguing that the war was a counter-revolutionary strike, fought between competing empires driven by the interests of industrial capitalism and used to avert escalating domestic problems, might also be supported by Casement's robust insights.[22]

The tendency to silence Casement in the narrative of his time has been achieved by a careful process of elision. A spate of revisionist biographies gradually diminished his intellectual stature, but his integrity managed to survive such assaults.[23] Casement has remained intrinsic to an extraordinarily active network of radical and progressive voices that were building alternative alliances of power that challenged the existing old order of the pre-First World War: a world of redundant monarchies and unrepresentative systems of oppressive power. His analysis of the system should be considered alongside other contemporaries who made similar challenges, notably Alice Stopford Green, James Connolly, Patrick Pearse, Nannie Dryhurst, Robert and Sylvia Lynd and HW Nevinson. He was very consciously building transnational solidarities linking the plight of the post-famine world of Ireland to the oppression experienced by the Quechan-speaking Andean communities to the violently exploited village on the upper Congo and the anti-colonial tide of resistance in India.

Perhaps his closest confidant in this struggle was the Irish historian, nationalist and feminist, Alice Stopford Green. Born in County Meath in 1847 and buried in Deansgrange Cemetery in May 1929,[24] Stopford Green remains one of the most underestimated and misconstrued figures of the revolutionary period. If one of the achievements of the commemoration of 2016 was to retrieve many key women involved in the cultural revival and revolutionary period back into the narrative, Stopford Green still remains an outsider. Yet the history she wrote in the years before 1916 was widely praised for uplifting the national spirit and had a considerable influence beyond Ireland in Britain and the U.S.[25]

From the first years of the twentieth century, the energetic collaboration of Stopford Green, Morel and Casement might be claimed as one of the most undervalued intellectual alliances of that era. In 1900, Stopford Green voyaged to South Africa to investigate the circumstances of the death of her friend, the ethnographer Mary Kingsley and to officially report on the conditions of Boer prisoners of war held in British camps on St Helena. On her return to London, she helped to launch the career of ED Morel, a young campaigner determined to carry on the work of Kingsley.

In early 1904, Green and Morel were joined in their efforts by Roger Casement, who had just returned from an official journey into the upper Congo to investigate the colonial regime of King Leopold II. By then Casement had survived almost twenty years in Africa and his official report would place him in the spotlight of imperial affairs. Between 1904 and 1914 Stopford Green, Morel and Casement collaborated closely on trying to reform the colonial system from within. Their coordinated criticism of empire required them to call into question notions of "civilization", colonial relations, the ethics of international capital, the circulation of modern armaments and the epistemology of empire. Stopford Green's histories of Ireland, Casement's investigation of the mistreatment of 'native' people, and Morel's vast body of work on affairs of West Africa are each and all intrinsic strands of the same progressive, and at times revolutionary, agenda. Infused with their hopes for a reform were remarkably modern concerns about corporate responsibility, fair trade, the ethics of the supply chain and greater transparency and accountability.

By 1911, their combined efforts had shifted towards the deepening crisis on the domestic front. Increasingly disillusioned by the trajectory of Liberal imperialism, they wound up their direct engagement with African and colonial affairs as they deepened their commitment to campaigning against the war. In 1913, the Congo Reform Association – the organisation established in 1904 to apply pressure to bring about reform – ceased operating. Morel focussed on widening his investigation of secret diplomacy and the culture of democratically unaccountable politics spinning the world towards Armageddon. Stopford Green and Casement channelled their energies into the Irish Volunteer movement. In May 1914, following the arming of the Ulster Volunteers the previous month, Stopford Green and Casement conspired with Erskine Childers and others to run guns into Ireland.[26] Those guns would arrive into Dublin and Kilcoole in late July as the world was being sucked towards that vortex of violent conflict that would ultimately define the course of the twentieth century.

The fate of Stopford Green, Casement and Morel would be changed utterly by the war. Casement's flight to Germany and his return to Ireland on board a submarine on the eve of the Easter Rising ended with his execution. Even the immense influence wielded by Stopford Green among her many friends in high places could not save her friend from the scaffold.

In 1917, Morel was imprisoned for a technical breach of the Defence of the Realm Act. His prison experience left him a broken man and though he would win a bitterly fought parliamentary seat against his arch-rival Winston Churchill in 1922, he died young in his early fifties burnt out by ceaseless campaigning.[27] In spite of his huge body of work dealing with both Africa and the diplomatic entanglements and deepening culture of secrecy that brought about the First World War, Morel has been sidelined in the public consciousness. Despite this marginalisation, he was a critical figure in the impetus that brought the Labour Party to power in 1924. The Union of Democratic Control would endure as a catalyst for an alternative discussion on international relations well into the 1960s.

Stopford Green survived the war but her life in London was made increasingly difficult. Her home on Grosvenor Road, a few minutes walk from the Houses of Parliament, became a refuge for those sympathetic to the on-going struggle for Irish independence. In 1921, sick and tired of the killing, she supported Michael Collins and the compromise over the settlement. She was one of four women elected to the first Irish senate and lived out the last years of her life in a house overlooking St. Stephen's Green. Her home was regularly raided by the security services and her papers confiscated. In her twilight years, she lectured and published widely on matters intended to facilitate the transition of Ireland towards stable, independent governance. Her death in May 1929 was attended by many of the most powerful dignitaries of the Irish Free State.

For Casement and Stopford Green, as their focus moved away from the colonial sphere to the deepening crisis in Ireland, they aspired to a unique vision for the nation once independence had been achieved. Through their various interventions, they strove to awaken a heightened sense of humanity and the possibility of an independent Irish foreign policy rooted in a global solidarity for those faced by the violent reality of colonial capitalism. In that often quoted line from his earliest surviving letter to Stopford Green, Casement wrote:

> the claim of the Congo people must appeal to every sincere and genuine Irish national: the more we love our land and wish to help her people the more keenly we feel we cannot turn a deaf ear to suffering and injustice in any part of the world.[28]

This deliberate fusion of the cause of Irish nationality in a bond of empathy with victims of violence and discrimination was a noble intention. In the case of Casement, such an affirmation was given real substance because of his own example: a life dedicated to revealing the excesses of his age, giving voice to the voiceless, and defending the right to rebellion.

The Crime against Europe endures as a shocking insight into the turmoil of those years that pushed the world over the edge and into a global war that would determine the course of the next century. From his trial notes and final letters, it is apparent that Casement considered these essays to be his own coherent summing up of the causes of war that could elucidate and justify his own paradigmatic shift in allegiances. In his brief to counsel, dictated when imprisoned in the Tower of London to his solicitor George Gavan Duffy, he commented: '*The Crime Against Europe* … states something of my views as to the responsibility for the war which I believed & believe to be well founded & demonstrable.'[29] He understood that while these essays would ultimately reveal his treason they would also explain the logic that led him to the scaffold on 3 August 1916:

> the 'Crime' is so damaging an exposure of English methods in Ireland & so strong an appeal to the right & duty of fighting for freedom that I am quite content to have the 'Crime' figure as the chief item against me – as in truth it is. If read in court & reported in the press it goes all over the world & it will in the end bring more converts to my cause than are dreamed of today.[30]

Perhaps because of these essays, Casement has found himself on the wrong side of history. Yet, in spite of the smear campaigns launched against him, his intellectual integrity has never been assailed. Like others involved in Ireland's cultural revival, he had a finely tuned sense of 'truth', closely bound up with his conviction in the power of the written word. His investigations in both sub-Saharan Africa and the Amazon had revealed 'things' that as Joseph Conrad famously commented: 'Things I've tried to forget; things I never did know.' He spoke truth to power with clarity and spirit that still disconcert; for, as he said on more than one occasion in his final months, 'it is only the truth that wounds'.[31]

© Angus Mitchell, 2017

Endnotes

1   *Documents Relevant to the Sinn Fein Movement, 1921* [Cd.1108].

2   First published as *The Crime against Ireland and How the War may Right it* (New York, 1914), the essays were not given specific titles in this collection. An introduction was dated 1 September 1914: Casement's fiftieth birthday. Much of the work for the initial run of these essays was undertaken with the support of John Devoy and the *Gaelic American*.

3   Sir Roger Casement, *Le Crime contre l'Europe* (Brussels: Veritas, 1916) was published by 'Veritas' in a print-run of 25,000 copies. The only extant copy survives in the Bibliotheque Royale. What happened to the other copies remains a mystery. For a useful note on the various editions see *Roger Casement: The Crime against Europe and The Crime against Ireland* (Belfast: Athol Books, 2003), 59-60.

4   TNA HO 144/1636/331643/32 holds a six page undated manuscript (apparently written in preparation for his trial) entitled 'Pamphlets, articles, letters etc of mine on Ireland against England or pro-German that may be brought against me – directly or indirectly.' This note gave detailed information on most of Casement's political writings, such as where and when they were published.

5   NLI MS 49,154/14 – Roger Casement to Eilis and Gertrude Bannister, 30 July 1916.

6   Pat Walsh, *Roger Casement on the Great War: a commentary* (Belfast: Athol Books, 2017), 10.

7   Margaret O'Callaghan, 'Ireland, Empire and British Foreign Policy: Roger Casement and the First World War.' *Breac: A Journal of Irish Studies*, April 2016. (Free access on-line)

8   H. Mackey (ed.), *The Crime against Europe: Writings and poems of Roger Casement* (Dublin: Fallon, 1958). This edition contained some other political essays by Casement but it still fell short of the extensive volume envisaged by Casement.

9   London School of Economics, E.D. Morel Papers, 15 September 1909.

10 This argument is well made by Andrew McGrath, 'Just War Theory in Roger Casement's *The Crime against Europe*', *Field Day Review*, 10 (2014), 91-99.

11 Roger Casement, *One Bold Deed of Open Treason: The Berlin Diary of Roger Casement (1914-16)* (Dublin: Merrion, 2016)

12 Much of this material from *The Continental Times* has been recently collected and republished in *Irish Foreign Affairs*, Vol. 10, Nos. 1-3, March / June / September 2017. See too Pat Walsh, *Roger Casement on the Great War: a commentary* (Athol Books, 2017).

13 See The National Archives (UK) HO 144/1636/331643/32a with Casement's Prison Papers and various drafts on his speech from the dock.

14 The dispute over the Black Diaries endures to this day and remains a sticking point in relations between London, Dublin and Belfast. For the most recent development of this ongoing saga see *History Ireland*, 24:4, July/August 2016.

15 The recent interventions by Paul Hyde on the manipulation of Casement's archive are particularly important in this regard, especially *The Casement Secret* http://www.decoding-casement.com/research-papers/the-casement-secret/.

16   Patrick Cockburn, 'The Easter Rising, my grand-father and the untold story of Sir Roger Casement', *Independent* (London), 1 April 2016; Martina Devlin, Casement, 'Black Diaries' and Black Arts', *Independent* (Ireland), 25 April 2016; Robert Fisk, 'It's sad but true that in colonial times our government was better at responding to human rights abuses abroad than it is now', *Independent* (UK), 5 August 2016; Aidan McQuade, 'Sir Roger Casement fought slavery and imperialism – and Britain executed him', *Left Foot Forward*, 3 August 2016.

17   Speech made by President Michael D. Higgins, 9 February 2017, Peruvian Ministry of Foreign Affairs, *When the gaze must not be averted: The testament for humanity in the universality of Roger Casement's humanitarian vision*.

18   Recent work on Morel includes Dean Pavlakis, *British Humanitarianism and the Congo Reform Movement 1896-1913* (Ashgate, 2015); David Mitchell, *The Politics of Dissent: A Biography of E.D. Morel* (Bristol, Silver Woods Books, 2014); Catherine Guinness, *Rubber Justice: Dr Harry Grattan Guinness and the Congo Reform Campaign* (Private Published, 2017)

19   To understand Casement's official and private lives during this period see my editions: *The Amazon Journal of Roger Casement* (Lilliput Press & Anaconda Editions, 1997) and *Sir Roger Casement's Heart of Darkness: The 1911 Documents* (Irish Manuscripts Commission, 2003).

20   This argument was most forthrightly articulated in his attack on the historian, diplomat and Liberal peer, James Bryce in 'The Far Extended Baleful Power of the Lie', published initially in *The Continental Times*, 3 November 1915, and republished as an appendix in Angus Mitchell, *Roger Casement: 16 Lives* (Dublin: The O'Brien Press, 2013).

21   See 'Protect Us from Our Protectors: Roger Casement, Imperialism, and Environmental Justice', in Eóin Flannery, *Ireland and Ecocriticism: Literature, History and Environmental Justic*e (Oxford: Routledge, 2016), 220-258.

22   Both Arno Mayer and Neil Faulkner have made measured Marxist readings of the war that might have benefitted from a closer reading of Casement. Mayer's thesis on the 'primacy of domestic politics' argues that Britain was on the brink of civil war in 1914 and this was averted by provoking a world war.

23   These include the works of Rene MacColl, H. Montgomery Hyde, Brian Inglis, B.L. Reid, Roger Sawyer, Jeffrey Dudgeon and Seamas Ó'Síocháin.

24   Ray Bateson, *Deansgrange Cemetery & The Easter Rising* (Irish Graves Publications, 2015), 131-32.

25   The most significant work in this regard was the controversial if highly original *The Making of Ireland and its Undoing* (Macmillan, 1908). In 1911, Stopford Green's popular historical survey *Irish Nationality* ran quickly into several editions and was read widely over the next decade. Her abilities as a historian and one prepared to take on the reactionary elements of the history profession is evident in *The Old Irish World* (Dublin: Gill & Macmillan, 1912).

26   F.X. Martin, *The Howth Gun-Running 1914* (Dublin: Browne and Nolan, 1964)

27   E.D. Morel, *Thoughts on the War: The Peace – and Prison* (Westminster: Privately Published, 1920)

28   NLI MS 10,464, RDC to ASG, 24 April 1904.

29   NLI MS 10,764.

30   NLI MS 10,764.

31   This is the opening sentence of his essay 'The Duty of Christendom', but the line also appears in his prison papers.

Chapter I

The Causes of the War and the Foundation of Peace

Since the war, foreshadowed in these pages, has come and finds public opinion in America gravely shocked at a war it believes to be solely due to certain phases of European militarism, the writer is now persuaded to publish these articles, which at least have the merit of having been written well before the event, in the hope that they may furnish a more useful point of view. For if one thing is certain it is that European militarism is no more the cause of this war than of any previous war. Europe is not fighting to see who has the best army, or to test mere military efficiency, but because certain peoples wish certain things and are determined to get and keep them by an appeal to force. If the armies and fleets were small the war would have broken out just the same, the parties and their claims, intentions, and positions being what they are. To find the causes of the war we must seek the motives of the combatants, and if we would have a lasting peace the foundations upon which to build it must be laid bare by revealing those foundations on which the peace was broken. To find the causes of the war we should turn not to Blue Books or White Papers, giving carefully selected statements of those responsible for concealing from the public the true issues that move nations to attack each other, but should seek the unavowed aims of those nations themselves.

Once the motive is found it is not hard to say who it is that broke the peace, whatever the diplomats may put forward in lieu of the real reason.

The war was, in truth, inevitable, and was made inevitable years ago. It was not brought about through the faults or temper of Sovereigns or their diplomats, not because there were great armies in Europe, but because certain Powers, and one Power in particular, nourished ambitions and asserted claims that involved not only ever increasing armaments but insured ever increasing animosities. In these cases peace, if permitted, would have dissipated the ambitions and upset claims, so it was only a question of time and opportunity when those whose aims required war would find occasion to bring it about.

As Mr. Bernard Shaw put it, in a recent letter to the press: "After having done all in our power to render war inevitable it is no use now to beg people not to make a disturbance, but to come to London to be kindly but firmly spoken to by Sir Edward Grey."

To find the motive powerful enough to have plunged all Europe into war in the short space of a few hours, we must seek it, not in the pages of a "white paper" covering a period of only fifteen days (July 20th to August 4th, 1914), but in the long anterior activities that led the great Powers of Europe into definite commitments to each other. For the purposes of this investigation we can eliminate at once three of the actual combatants, as being merely "accessories after the fact," viz.: - Servia, Belgium and Japan, and confine our study of the causes of the conflict to the aims and motives of the five principal combatants. For it is clear that in the quarrel between Servia and Austria, Hungary is only a side issue of the larger question that divides Europe into armed camps. Were categoric proof sought of how small a part the quarrel between Vienna and Belgrade played in the larger tragedy, it can be found in the urgent insistence of the Russian Government itself in the very beginning of the diplomatic conversations that preceded the outbreak of hostilities.

As early as the 24th of July, the Russian Government sought to prevail upon Great Britain to proclaim its complete solidarity with Russia and France, and on the British Ambassador in St. Petersburg pointing out that "direct British interests in Servia were nil, and a war on behalf of that country would never be sanctioned by British public opinion," the Russian Minister of Foreign Affairs replied that "we must not forget that the general European question was involved, the Servian question being but a part of the former, and that Great Britain could not afford to efface herself from the problem now at issue." *(Despatch of Sir G. Buchanan to Sir E. Grey, 24th July, 1914).*

Those problems involved far mightier questions than the relations of Servia to Austria, the neutrality of Belgium or the wish of Japan to keep the peace of the East by seizing Kiao-Chau.

The neutrality never became a war issue until long after war had been decided on and had actually broken out; while Japan came into the contest solely because Europe had obligingly provided one, and because one European power preferred, for its own ends, to strengthen an Asiatic race to seeing a kindred white people it feared grow stronger in the sun.

Coming then to the five great combatants, we can quickly reduce them to four. Austria-Hungary and Germany in this war are indivisible. While each may have varying aims on many points and ambitions that, perhaps, widely diverge both have one common bond, self-preservation, that binds them much more closely together than mere formal "allies." In this war Austria fights of necessity as a Germanic Power, although the challenge to her has been on the ground of her Slav obligations and activities. Germany is compelled to support Austria by a law of necessity that a glance at the map of Europe explains. Hence, for the purpose of the argument, we may put the conflict as between the Germanic peoples of Central Europe and those who have quarreled with them.

We thus arrive at the question, "why should such strangely consorted allies as England, Russia and France be at war with the German people?"

The answer is not to be found in the White Book, or in any statement publicly put forward by Great Britain, Russia or France.

But the answer must be found, if we would find the causes of the war, and if we would hope to erect any lasting peace on the ruins of this world conflict.

To accept, as an explanation of the war the statement that Germany has a highly trained army she has not used for nearly half a century and that her people are so obsessed with admiration for it that they longed to test it on their neighbours, is to accept as an explanation a stultifying contradiction. It is of course much easier to put the blame on the Kaiser. This line of thought is highly popular: it accords, too, with a fine vulgar instinct.

The German people can be spared the odium of responsibility for a war they clearly did nothing to provoke, by representing them as the victims of an autocracy, cased in mail and beyond their control. We thus arrive at "the real crime against Germany," which explains everything but the thing it set out to explain. It leaves unexplained the real crime against Europe.

To explain the causes of the war we must find the causes of the alliances of England, France and Russia against Germany.

For the cause of the war is that alliance that and nothing else. The defence of the *Entente Cordiale* is that it is an innocent pact of friendship, designed only to meet the threat of the Triple Alliance. But the answer to that is that whereas the Triple Alliance was formed thirty years ago, it has never declared war on anyone, while the Triple Entente before it is eight years old has involved Europe, America, Africa, and Asia in a world conflict. We must find the motive for England allying herself with France and Russia in an admittedly anti-German "understanding" if we would understand the causes of the present war and why it is that many besides Bernard Shaw hold that "after having done all in our power to render war inevitable" it was idle for the British Government to assume a death-bed solicitude for peace, having already dug its grave and cast aside the shovel for the gun. When that motive is apparent we shall realise who it was preferred war to peace and how impossible it is to hope for any certain peace ensuing from the victory of those who ensured an appeal to arms.

The *Entente Cordiale*, to begin with, is unnatural. There is nothing in common between the parties to it, save antagonism to someone else. It is wrongly named. It is founded not on predilections but on prejudices - not on affection but on animosity. To put it crudely it is a bond of hate not of love. None of the parties to it like or admire each other, or have consistent aims, save one.

That satisfied, they will surely fall out among themselves, and the greater the plunder derived from their victory the more certain their ensuing quarrel.

Great Britain, in her dealings with most white people (not with all) is a democracy.

Russia in her dealings with all, is an autocracy.

Great Britain is democratic in her government of herself and in her dealings with the great white communities of Canada, Australia, New Zealand, and South Africa. She is not democratic in her dealings with subject races within the Empire - the Indians, notably, or the Irish. To the Indians her rule is that of an absentee autocracy, differing in speech, colour, religion and culture from those submitted to it by force; to the Irish that of a resident autocracy bent on eliminating the people governed from residence in their own country, and replacing them with cattle for British consumption.

In both instances Britain is notably false to her professions of devotion to democratic principles. Her affinity with Russia is found then, not in the cases where her institutions are good, but in those where they are bad.

An alliance founded on such grounds of contact can only produce evil.

To such it gave birth in Persia, to such it must give birth in the present war.

In Persia we saw it betray the principles of democratic government, destroy an infant constitution and disembowel the constitutionalists, whilst it divided their country into "spheres of influence" and to-day we see it harvesting with hands yet red with the blood of Persian patriots the redder fruit of the seed then sown.

The alliance with France, while more natural than that with Russia if we regard Great Britain as a democracy (by eliminating India, Egypt, Ireland) had the same guilty end in view, and rests less on affinity of aims than on affinity of antipathies.

The *Entente Cordiale*, the more closely we inspect it, we find is based not on a cordial regard of the parties to it for each other, but on a cordial disregard all three participants share for the party it is aimed against.

It will be said that Germany must have done something to justify the resentment that could bring about so strangely assorted a combination against herself. What has been the crime of Germany against the powers now assailing her? She has doubtless committed many crimes, as have all the great powers, but in what respect has she so grievously sinned against Europe that the Czar, the Emperor of India, the King of Great Britain and Ireland, the Mikado and the President of the French Republic to say nothing of those minor potentates who like Voltaire's minor prophets seem *capable de tout* should now be pledged, by irrevocable pact, to her destruction as a great power?

"German militarism," the reply that springs to the lips, is no more a threat to civilisation than French or Russian militarism. It was born, not of wars of aggression, but of wars of defence and unification. Since it was welded by blood and iron into the great human organism of the last forty years it has not been employed beyond the frontiers of Germany until last year.

Can the same be said of Russian militarism or of French militarism or of British navalism?

We are told the things differ in quality. The answer is what about the intent and the uses made. German militarism has kept peace and has not emerged beyond its own frontier until threatened with universal attack. Russian militarism has waged wars abroad, far beyond the confines of Russian territory; French militarism, since it was overthrown at Sedan, has carried fire and sword across all Northern Africa, has penetrated from the Atlantic to the Nile, has raided Tonquin, Siam, Madagascar, Morocco, while English navalism in the last forty years has bombarded the coast lines, battered the ports, and landed raiding parties throughout Asia and Africa, to say nothing of the well nigh continuous campaigns of annexation of the British army in India, Burma, South Africa, Egypt, Tibet, or Afghanistan, within the same period.

As to the quality of the materialism of the great Continental Powers there is nothing to prefer in the French and Russian systems to the German system. Each involved enormous sacrifices on the people sustaining it. We are asked, however, to believe that French militarism is maintained by a "democracy" and German militarism by an "autocracy." Without appealing to the captive Queen of Madagascar for an opinion on the authenticity of French democracy we may confine the question to the elected representatives of the two peoples.

In both cases the war credits are voted by the legislative bodies responsible to French and German opinion. The elected representatives of Germany are as much the spokesman of the nation as those of France, and the German Reichstag has sanctioned every successive levy for the support of German armaments. As to Russian militarism, it may be presumed no one will go quite so far as to assert that the Russian Duma is more truly representative of the Russian people than the Parliament of the Federated peoples of Germany at Berlin.

The machines being then approximately the same machines, we must seek the justification for them in the uses to which they have been put.

For what does France, for what does Russia maintain a great army? Why does Germany call so many youthful Germans to the colours? On what grounds of moral sanction does Great Britain maintain a navy, whose cost far exceeds all the burdens of German militarism?

Russia stretches across the entire area of Central Asia and comprises much of the greater part of Europe as well. In its own territory, it is unassailable, and never has been invaded with success. No power can plunder or weaken Russia as long as she remains within her own borders. Of all the great powers in Europe she is the one that after England has the least need of a great army. She cannot be assailed with success at home, and she has no need to leave her own territories in search of lands to colonize. Her population, secure in its own vast numbers and vast resources has, for all future needs of expansion the continent of Siberia into which to overflow. Russia cannot be threatened within Russia and has no need to go outside Russia. A Russian army of 4,000,000 is not necessary to self-defence. Its inspiration can be due only to a policy of expansion at the cost of others, and its aim to extend and to maintain existing Russian frontiers. As I write it is engaged not in a war of defence but in a war of invasion, and is the instrument of a policy of avowed aggression.

Not the protection of the Slavs from Austria, herself so largely a Slavic power and one that does not need to learn the principles of good government from Russia, but the incorporation of the Slavs within the mightiest empire upon earth - this is the main reason why Russia maintains the mightiest army upon earth. Its threat to Germany, as the protector of Austria-Hungary, has been clear, and if we would find the reason for German militarism we shall find at least one half of it across the Russian frontier.

The huge machine of the French army, its first line troops almost equal to Germany's, is not a thing of yesterday.

It was not German aggression founded it - although Germany felt it once at Jena. Founded by kings of France, French militarism has flourished under republic, empire, constitutional monarchy, and empire again until to-day we find its greatest bloom full blown under the mild breath of the third republic. What is the purpose of this perfect machine? Self-defence? From what attack? Germany has had it in her power, again and again within the last thirty years to attack France at a disadvantage, if not even with impunity. Why has she refrained - whose hand restrained her? Not Russia's - not England's. During the Russo-Japanese war or during the Boer war, France could have been assailed with ease and her army broken to pieces. But German militarism refrained from striking that blow. The object of the great army France maintains is not to be found in reasons of self-defence, but may be found, like that of Russia in hopes of armed expansion. Since the aim in both cases was the same, to wage a war of aggression to be termed of "recovery" in one case and "protection" in the other, it was not surprising that Czar and President should come together, and that the cause of the Slavs should become identified with the cause of Strasburg.

To "protect" the Slavs meant assailing Austria-Hungary (another way of attacking Germany), and to "recover" Strasburg meant a *mes-alliance* between democrat of France and Cossack of the Don.

We come now to the third party to die Entente, and it is now we begin to perceive how it was that a cordial understanding with England rendered a Russo-French attack upon Germany only a question of time and opportunity. Until England appeared upon the scene neither Russia nor France, nor both combined, could summon up courage to strike the blow. Willing to wound they were both afraid to strike. It needed a third courage, a keener purpose and a greater immunity.

German militarism was too formidable a factor in the life of 65,000,000 of the most capable people in Europe to be lightly assailed even by France and Russia combined. Russia needed money to perfect the machinery of invasion, so sorely tried by the disastrous failure to invade Korea and Manchuria. France had the money to advance, but she still doubted the ability of her stagnant population of 40,000,000 to face the growing magnitude of the great people across the Rhine. It needed another guarantee - and England brought it.

From the day that Great Britain and her mighty fleet joined the separated allies with their mighty armies, the bond between them and the circle round Germany grew taut. From that day the counsels of the allies and their new found "friend" thickened and quickened. The immovable "menace across the Rhine" in one case had become the active "menace across the North Sea" in the other case.

The sin of German militarism was at last out. It could take to the water as kindly as to the land. As long as the war machine guaranteed the inviolability of German territory it was no threat to European peace, but when it assumed the task of safe-guarding German rights at sea it became the enemy of civilization. These trading people not content with an army that kept French "revanche" discreetly silent and Slav "unity" a dream of the future presumed to have a sea-born commerce that grew by leaps and bounds, and they dared to build a navy to defend and even to extend it. *Delenda est Carthago!* From that day the doom of "German militarism" was sealed; and England, democratic England, lay down with the Czar in the same bed to which the French housewife had already transferred her republican counterpane.

The duration of peace became only a question of time, and the war of to-day only a question of opportunity and pretext. Each of the parties to the understanding had the same clear purpose to serve, and while the aim to each was different the end was the same. Germany's power of defence must be destroyed. That done each of the sleeping partners to the unsigned compact would get the share of the spoils, guarded by armed German manhood, he coveted.

To Russia, the dismemberment of Austria-Hungary and the incorporation of the Slav elements in part into her own vast empire, in part into a vassal and subordinate Balkan Confederacy.

To France the restoration of Lorraine, with Metz, and of Alsace with Strasburg and their 1,500,000 of German speaking Teutons to the French Empire.

To England, the destruction of German sea-power and along with it the permanent crippling of German competition in the markets of the world.

Incidentally German colonies would disappear along with German shipping, and with both gone a German navy would become a useless burden for a nation of philosophers to maintain, so that the future status of maritime efficiency in Europe could be left to the power that polices the seas to equitably fix for all mankind, as well as for the defeated rival.

Such an outline was the altruistic scope of the unsigned agreement entered into by the three parties of the *Triple Entente*; and it only remained to get ready for the day when the matter could be brought to issue. The murder of the Archduke Ferdinand furnished Russia with the occasion, since she felt that her armies were ready, the sword sharpened, and the Entente sure and binding.

The mobilization by Russia was all that France needed "to do that which might be required of her by her interests." (Reply of the French Government to the German Ambassador at Paris, August 1st, 1914.)

Had the neutrality of Belgium been respected as completely as the neutrality of Holland, England would have joined her "friends" in the assault on Germany, as Sir Edward Grey was forced to admit when the German Ambassador in vain pressed him to state his own terms as the price of English neutrality.

The hour had struck. Russia was sure of herself, and the rest followed automatically since all had been provided for long before. The French fleet was in the Mediterranean, as the result of the military compact between France and England signed, sealed and delivered in November, 1912, and *withheld from the cognizance of the British Parliament until after war had been declared*. The British fleet had been mobilized early in July in anticipation of Russia's mobilization on land - and here again it is Sir Edward Grey who incidentally supplies the proof.

In his anxiety, while there was still the fear that Russia might hold her hand, he telegraphed to the British Ambassador in St. Petersburg on 27th of July, requiring him to assure the Russian Foreign Minister, that the British Fleet, "which is concentrated, *as it happens*" would not disperse from Portland.

That "as it happens" is quite the most illuminating slip in the British White Paper, and is best comprehended by those who know what have been the secret orders of the British fleet since 1909, and what was the end in view when King George reviewed it earlier in the month, and when His Majesty so hurriedly summoned the unconstitutional "Home Rule" conference at Buckingham Palace on 18th of July. Nothing remained for the "friends" but to so manoeuvre that Germany should be driven to declare war, or see her frontiers crossed. If she did the first, she became the "aggressor"; if she waited to be attacked she incurred the peril of destruction.

Such, in outline, are the causes and steps that led to the outbreak of war. The writer has seen those steps well and carefully laid, tested and tried beforehand. Every rung of the scaling ladder being raised for the storming of the German defences on land and sea was planed and polished in the British Foreign Office.

As Sir Edward Grey confessed three years ago, he was "but the fly on the wheel." That wheel was the ever faster driven purpose of Great Britain to destroy the growing sea-power and commerce of Germany. The strain had reached the breaking point.

During the first six months of 1914, German export trade almost equalled that of Great Britain. Another year of peace, and it would certainly have exceeded it, and for the first time in the history of world trade Great Britain would have been put in the second place. German exports from January to June had swelled to the enormous total of $1,045,000,000 as against the $1,075,000,000 of Great Britain. A war against such figures could not be maintained in the markets, it must be transferred to the seas.

Day by day as the war proceeds, although it is now only six weeks old, the pretences under which it was begun are being discarded. England fights not to defend the neutrality of Belgium, not to destroy German militarism, but to retain, if need be by involving the whole world in war, her supreme and undisputed ownership of the seas.

This is the crime against Europe, the crime against the world that, among other victims the United States are invited to approve, in order that to-morrow their own growing navy may be put into a like posture with that of a defeated Germany.

With the Kiel Canal "handed to Denmark," as one of the fruits of British victory, as Lord Charles Beresford yesterday magnanimously suggested, how long may it be before the Panama Canal shall be found to be "a threat to peace" in the hands of those who constructed it?

A rival fleet in being, whether the gunners be Teuton or Anglo-Saxon unless the Admiralty controlling it is seated at Whitehall, will always be an eyesore to the Mistress of the seas, in other words, "a threat to the peace of the world."

The war of armaments cannot be ended by the disarming of the German people. To hand Europe over to a triumphal alliance of Russian and French militarism, while England controls the highways and waterways of mankind by a fleet whose function is "to dictate the maritime law of nations," will beget indeed a new Europe, but a Europe whose acquiescence is due to fear and the continued pressure of well-sustained force - a Europe submitted to the despotism of unnatural alliances designed to arrest the laws of progress.

The laws of progress demand that efficiency shall prevail. The crime of Germany has been superior efficiency, not so much in the arts of war as in the products of peace. If she go down to-day before a combination of brute force and unscrupulous intelligence her fall cannot be permanent. Germany has within herself the forces that ensure revival, and revival means recovery. Neither France nor Russia nor both combined, can give to Europe what Britain now designs to take from it by their help.

Whatever may be the result of this war on the field of battle, to France indeed it can bring only one end. For her there is no future save that of a military empire. Her life blood is dried up. This war will sweep away all power of recuperation. She will remain impotent to increase her race, sterile of new forces for good, her young men's blood gone to win the barren fields of Alsace. Her one purpose in the new Europe will be to hold a sword, not her own, over the struggling form of a resurgent Germany in the interests of another people. Let Germany lose 1,000,000 men in the fighting of to-day, she can recover them in two years of peace. But to France the losses of this war, whether she win or lose, cannot be made good in a quarter of a century of child births. Whatever comes to Russia, to England, France as a great free power is gone. Her future function will be to act in a subordinate capacity alone; supported and encouraged by England she will be forced to keep up a great army in order that the most capable people of the continent, with a population no defeat can arrest, shall not fill the place in Europe and in the world they are called on surely to fill, and one that conflicts only with British aims and appetites.

German expansion was no threat to France. It was directed to other fields, chiefly those of commerce. In order to keep it from those fields England fanned the dying fires of French resentment and strove by every agency to kindle a natural sentiment into an active passion.

The historian of the future will record that whatever the immediate fate of Germany may be, the permanent victim was France.

The day England won her to an active policy of vengeance against the victor of 1870, she wooed her to abiding loss. Her true place in Europe was one of friendship with Germany. But that meant, inevitably, the discovery by Europe that the chief barrier to European concord lay not in the armies of the powers, but in the ring of hostile battleships that constrained her peoples into armed camps.

European militarism rests on English navalism. English navalism requires for its continued existence a disunited Europe; and a Europe kept apart is a Europe armed, anxious and watchful, bent on mutual attack, its eyes fixed on the earth. Europe must lift its eyes to the sea. There lies the highway of the nations, the only road to freedom - the sole path to peace.

For the pent millions of Europe there can be no peace, no laying aside of arms, no sincere development of trade or culture while one people, *in Europe but not of Europe*, immune themselves from all attack, and sure that whatever suffering they inflict on others can never be visited on their own shores, have it in their power to foment strife with impunity and to call up war from the ends of the earth while they themselves enjoy the blessing of peace.

England, the soul and brain of this confederacy of war abroad remains at peace at home. As I write these words a despatch from Sir Alfred Sharpe, the correspondent of a London paper in France, comes to hand. It should be placarded in every Foreign Office of the world, in every temple of justice, in every house of prayer.

> "It is difficult for the people in England to realize the condition of Northern France at the present time. Although the papers are full of accounts of desolation and destruction caused by the German invasion, it is only by an actual experience that a full realization of the horror comes. To return to England after visiting the French war zone is to come back to a land of perfect peace, where everything is normal and where it is not easy to believe we are almost within hearing distance of the cannonade on the Aisne."
> (Sir Alfred Sharpe, to the *Daily Chronicle* from the Front, September 2nd, 1914.)

It is this immunity from the horror of war that makes all Englishmen jingoes. They are never troubled by the consequences of belligerency. Since it is only by "an actual experience that the full realization of the horror comes." Until that horror strikes deep on English soil her statesmen, her Ministers, her Members of Parliament, her editors, will never sincerely love peace, but will plan always to ensure war abroad, whenever British need or ambition demands it.

Were England herself so placed that responsibility for her acts could be enforced on her own soil, among her own people, and on the head of those who devise her policies, then we might talk of arbitration treaties with hope, and sign compacts of goodwill sure that they were indeed cordial understandings.

But as long as Great Britain retains undisputed ownership of the chief factor that ensures at will peace or war on others, there can be only armaments in Europe, ill-will among men and war fever in the blood of mankind.

British democracy loves freedom of the sea in precisely the same spirit as imperial Rome viewed the spectacle of Celtic freedom beyond the outposts of the Roman legions; as Agricola phrased it, something "to wear down and take possession of so that freedom may be put out of sight."

The names change but the spirit of imperial exploitation, whether it call itself an empire or a democracy, does not change.

Just as the Athenian Empire, in the name of a democracy, sought to impose servitude at sea on the Greek world, so the British Empire, in the name of a democracy, seeks to encompass mankind within the long walls of London.

The modern Sparta may be vanquished by the imperial democrats assailing her from East and West. But let the world be under no illusions.

If Germany go down to-day, vanquished by a combination of Asiatic, African, American, Canadian and European enemies, the gain will not be to the world nor to the cause of peace.

The mistress of the seas will remain to ensure new combinations of enmity to prohibit the one league of concord that alone can bring freedom and peace to the world. The cause that begot this war will remain to beget new wars.

The next victim of universal sea-power may not be on the ravaged fields of mid-Europe, but mid the wasted coasts and bombarded seaports of the Atlantic and Pacific Oceans.

A permanent peace can only be laid on a sure foundation. A sure foundation of peace among men can only be found when mastery of the sea by one people has been merged in freedom of the seas for all.

Chapter II

The Keeper of the Seas

As long ago as 1870 an Irishman pointed out that if the English press did not abandon the campaign of prejudiced suspicion it was even then conducting against Germany, the time for an understanding between Great Britain and the German people would be gone for ever.

It was Charles Lever who delivered this shrewd appreciation of the onlooker.

Writing from Trieste on August 29th, 1870, to John Blackwood, he stated:

> "Be assured the *Standard* is making a great blunder by its anti-Germanism and English opinion has just now a value in Germany which if the nation be once disgusted with us will be gone for ever."

Lever preserved enough of the Irishman through all his official connection to see the two sides of a question and appreciate the point of view of the other man.

What Lever pointed out during the early stages of the Franco-German war has come to pass. The *Standard* of forty years ago is the British press of to-day, with here and there the weak voice of an impotent Liberalism crying in the wilderness. Germany has, indeed, become thoroughly disgusted and the hour of reconciliation has long since gone by. In Lever's time it was now or never; the chance not taken then would be lost for ever, and the English publicist of to-day is not in doubt that it is now too late. His heart-searchings need another formula of expression no longer a conditional assertion of doubt, but a positive questioning of impending fact, "is it too soon." That the growing German navy must be smashed he is convinced, but how or when to do it he is not so clear.

The situation is not yet quite intolerable, and so, although many urge an immediate attack before the enemy grows too strong, the old-time British love of compromise and trust in luck still holds his hand. The American "alliance" too, may yet come off. The Entente with France, already of great value, can be developed into something more assuredly anti-German, and if present-day relations of friendship with the United States can be but tightened into a mutual committal of both Powers to a common foreign policy, then the raid on Germany may never be needed. She can be bottled up without it. No man who studies the British mind can have any doubt of the fixed trend of British thought.

It can be summed up in one phrase. German expansion is not to be tolerated. It can only be a threat to or attained at the expense of British interests. Those interests being world-wide, with the seas for their raiment nay, with the earth for their footstool it follows that wherever Germany may turn for an outlet she is met by the British challenge: "Not there!" British interests interdict the Old World; the Monroe Doctrine, maintained, it is alleged by British naval supremacy, forbids the New.

Let Germany acquire a coaling station, a sanitorium, a health resort, the ground for a hotel even, on some foreign shore, and "British interests" spring to attention, English jealousy is aroused. How long this state of tension can last without snapping could, perhaps, be best answered in the German naval yards. It is evident that some 7,000,000 of the best educated race in the world, physically strong, mentally stronger, homogeneous, highly trained, highly skilled, capable and energetic and obedient to a discipline that rests upon and is moulded by a lofty conception of patriotism, cannot permanently be confined to a strictly limited area by a less numerous race, less well educated, less strong mentally and physically and assuredly less well trained, skilled and disciplined. Stated thus the problem admits of a simple answer; and were there no other factor governing the situation, that answer would have been long since given.

It is not the ethical superiority of the English race that accounts for their lead, but the favourable geographical situation from which they have been able to develop and direct their policy of expansion.

England has triumphed mainly from her position. The qualities of her people have, undoubtedly, counted for much, but her unrivalled position in the lap of the Atlantic, barring the seaways and closing the tideways of Central and North-eastern Europe, has counted for more.

With this key she has opened the world to herself and closed it to her rivals.

The long wars with France ended in the enhancement of this position by the destruction of the only rival fleet in being.

Europe, without navies, without shipping became for England a mere westward projection of Asia, dominated by warlike peoples who could always be set by the ears and made to fight upon points of dynastic honour, while England appropriated the markets of mankind. Thenceforth, for the best part of a century, while Europe was spent in what, to the superior Britain were tribal conflicts, the seas and coasts of the world lay open to the intrusions of his commerce, his colonists, his finance, until there was seemingly nothing left outside the two Americas worth laying hands on. This highly favoured maritime position depends, however, upon an unnamed factor, the unchallenged possession and use of which by England has been the true foundation of her imperial greatness.

Without Ireland there would be to-day no British Empire. The vital importance of Ireland to England is understood, but never proclaimed by every British statesman. To subdue that western and ocean-closing island and to exploit its resources, its people and, above all its position, to the sole advantage of the eastern island, has been the set aim of every English Government from the days of Henry VIII onwards. The vital importance of Ireland to Europe is not and has not been understood by any European statesman.

To them it has not been a European island, a vital and necessary element of European development, but an appanage of England, an island beyond an island, a mere geographical expression in the titles of the conqueror. Louis XIV, came nearest, perhaps, of European rulers to realizing its importance in the conflict of European interests when he sought to establish James II on its throne as rival to the monarch of Great Britain and counterpoise to the British sovereignty in the western seas. Montesquieu alone of French writers grasped the importance of Ireland in the international affairs of his time, and he blames the vacillation of Louis, who failed to put forth his strength, to establish James upon the throne of Ireland and thus by a successful act of perpetual separation to *affaiblir le voisin*. Napoleon, too late, in St. Helena, realized his error: "Had I gone to Ireland instead of to Egypt the Empire of England was at an end."

With these two utterances of the French writer and of the French ruler we begin and end the reference of Ireland to European affairs which continental statecraft has up to now emitted, and so far has failed to apply.

To-day there is probably no European thinker (although Germany produced one in recent times), who, when he faces the over-powering supremacy of Great Britain's influence in world affairs and the relative subordination of European rights to the asserted interests of that small island, gives a thought to the other and smaller island beyond its shores. And yet the key to British supremacy lies there. Perhaps the one latter day European who perceived the true relation of Ireland to Great Britain was Neibuhr.

"Should England," he said, "not change her conduct, Ireland may still for a long period belong to her, but not always; and the loss of that country is the death day, not only to her greatness, but of her very existence."

I propose to point out as briefly as may be possible in dealing with so unexpected a proposition, that the restoration of Ireland to European life lies at the bottom of all successful European effort to break the bonds that now shackle every continental people that would assert itself and extend its ideals, as opposed to British interests, outside the limits of Europe.

It may be well first to define "British interests" and to show that these are not necessarily synonymous with European interests. British interests are: first, the control of all the seas of all the world in full military and commercial control. If this be not challenged peace is permitted: to dispute it seriously means war.

Next in order of British interests stands the right of pre-emption to all healthy, fertile, "unoccupied" lands of the globe not already in possession of a people capable of seriously disputing invasion, with the right of reversion to such other regions as may, from time to time prove commercially desirable or financially exploitable, whether suitable for British colonization or not.

In a word, British interests assume that the future of the world shall be an English-speaking future. It is clear that sooner or later the British colonies, so called, must develop into separate nationalities, and that the link of a common crown cannot bind them forever. But, as Sir Wilfred Laurier said at the recent Imperial Conference: "We bring you British institutions" – English language, English law, English trade, English supremacy, in a word – this is the ideal reserved for mankind and summed up in words "British interests."

Turn where you will these interests are in effective occupation, and whether it be Madeira, Teneriffe, Agadir, Tahiti, Bagdad, the unseen flag is more potent to exclude the non-British intruder than the visible standard of the occupying tenant. England is the landlord of civilization, mankind her tenantry, and the earth her estate. If this be not a highly exaggerated definition of British interests, and in truth it is but a strongly coloured chart of the broad outline of the design, then it is clear that Europe has a very serious problem to face if European civilization and ideals, as differing from the British type, are to find a place for their ultimate expansion in any region favoured by the sun.

The actual conflict of European interests in Morocco is a fair illustration of English methods.[1]

In the past France was the great antagonist, but since she is to-day no longer able to seriously dispute the British usufruct of the overseas world she is used (and rewarded) in the struggle now maintained to exclude Germany at all costs from the arena. Were France still dangerous she would never have been allowed to go to Algeciras, or from Algeciras to Fez. She has uses, however, in the anti-German prize ring and so Morocco is the price of her hire. That Germany should presume to inspect the transaction or claim a share in the settlement has filled the British mind with profound indignation, the echoes of which are heard rumbling round the world from the Guildhall to Gaboon and from the Congo to Tahiti. The mere press rumour that France might barter Tahiti for German goods filled the British newspaper world with supermundane wrath. That France should presume to offer or Germany should accept a French Pacific island in part discharge of liabilities contracted at Algeciras was a threat to British interests. Tahiti in the hands of a decadent republic, the greatest if you will, but still one of the dying nations, is a thing to be borne with, but Tahiti possibly in the hands of Germany becomes at once a challenge and a threat.

And so we learn that "Australasia protests" to the Home Government at the mere rumour that France may choose to part with one of her possessions to win German goodwill in Morocco. Neither France nor Germany can be permitted to be a free agent in a transaction that however regarded as essential to their own interests might affect, even by a shadow on the sea, the world orbit of British interests. These interests it will be noted have reached such a stage of development as to require that all foreign States that cannot be used as tools, or regarded as agencies, must be treated as enemies. Germany with her growing population, her advancing industries, her keen commercial ability, and

1   This was written in August, 1911

her ever expanding navy has become the enemy of civilization. Far too strong to be openly assailed on land she must at all costs be pent up in Central Europe and by a ring-fence of armed understandings prohibited from a wider growth that would certainly introduce a rival factor to those British institutions and that world language that are seriously if not piously meditated as the ordained future for mankind.

For English mentality is such that whatever England does is divinely ordained, and whether she stamps out a nation or merely sinks a ship the hymn of action is "Nearer My God, to Thee." In a recent deputation to King George V it will be remembered that certain British religious bodies congratulated that monarch on the third centenary of the translation into English of the Bible.

Both the addresses of the subjects, eminent, religious and cultured men, and the sovereign's reply were highly informative of the mental attitude of this extraordinary people. The Bible, it appeared, was the "greatest possession of the English race." "The British Bible" was the first and greatest of British investments and upon the moral dividends derived from its possession was founded the imperial greatness of this Island Empire. That other peoples possessed the Bible and had even translated it before England was not so much as hinted at. That the Bible was Greek and Hebrew in origin was never whispered. It began and ended with the English Authorised Version. The British Bible was the Bible that counted. It was the Bible upon which the sun never sets, the Bible that had blown Indian mutineers from its muzzle in the 'fifties and was prepared to-day to have a shot at any other mutineers, Teuton or Turk, who dared to dispute its claim that the meek shall inherit the earth. The unctuous rectitude that converts the word of God into wadding for a gun is certainly a formidable opponent, as Cromwell proved.

To challenge English supremacy becomes not merely a threat to peace, it is an act of sacrilege. And yet this world-wide empire broad based upon the British Bible and the English navy, and maintained by a very inflexible interpretation of the one and a very skilful handling of the other, rests upon a sunk foundation that is older than both and will surely bring both to final shipwreck.

The British Empire is founded not upon the British Bible or the British dreadnought but upon Ireland. The empire that began upon an island, ravaged, sacked and plundered shall end on an island, "which whether it proceed from the very genius of the soil, or the influence of the stars, or that Almighty God hath not yet appointed the time of her reformation, or that He reserveth her in this unquiet state still for some secret scourge which shall by her come unto England, it is hard to be known but yet much to be feared." Thus Edmund Spenser 340 years ago, whose muse drew profit from an Irish estate (one of the first fruits of empire) and who being a poet had imagination to perceive that a day of payment must some day be called and that the first robbed might be the first to repay.

The Empire founded on Ireland by Henry and Elizabeth Tudor has expanded into mighty things. England deprived of Ireland resumes her natural proportions, those of a powerful kingdom. Still possessing Ireland she is always an empire. For just as Great Britain bars the gateways of northern and west central Europe, to hold up at will the trade and block the ports of every coast from the Baltic to the Bay of Biscay, so Ireland stands between Britain and the greater seas of the west and blocks for her the highways of the ocean.

An Ireland strong, independent and self-contained, a member of the European family of nations, restored to her kindred, would be the surest guarantee for the healthy development of European interests in those regions whence they are to-day excluded by the anti-European policy of England.

The relation of Ireland to Great Britain has been in no wise understood on the continent. The policy of England has been for centuries to conceal the true source of her supplies and to prevent an audit of transactions with the remoter island. As long ago as the reign of Elizabeth Tudor this shutting off of Ireland from contact with Europe was a settled point of English policy. The three "German Earls" with letters from the Queen who visited Dublin in 1572 were prevented by the Lord Deputy from seeing for themselves anything beyond the walls of the city.[2]

To represent the island as a poverty striken land inhabited by a turbulent and ignorant race whom she has with unrewarded solicitude sought to civilise, uplift and educate has been a staple of England's diplomatic trade since modern diplomacy began. To compel the trade of Ireland to be with herself alone; to cut off all direct communication between Europe and this second of European islands until no channel remained save through Britain; to enforce the most abject political and economic servitude one people ever imposed upon another; to exploit all Irish resources, lands, ports, people, wealth, even her religion, everything in fine that Ireland held, to the sole profit and advancement of England, and to keep all the books and rigorously refuse an audit of the transaction has been the secret but determined policy of England.

We have read lately something of Mexican peonage, of how a people can be reduced to a lawless slavery, their land expropriated, their bodies enslaved, their labour appropriated, and how the nexus of this fraudulent connection lies in a falsified account. The hacenade holds the peon by a debt bondage. His palace in Mexico City, or on the sisal plains of Yucatan is reared on the stolen labour of a people whose bondage is based on a lie. The hacenade keeps the books and debits the slave with the cost of the lash that scourges him into the fields. Ireland is the English peon, the great peon of the British Empire. The books and the palaces are in London but the work and the wealth have come from peons on the Irish Estate.

The armies that overthrew Napoleon; the fleets that swept the navies of France and Spain from the seas were recruited from this slave pen of English civilisation. During the last 100 years probably 2,000,000 Irishmen have been drafted into the English fleets and armies from a land purposely drained of its food. Fully the same number, driven by executive-controlled famines have given cheap labour to England and have built up her great industries, manned her shipping, dug her mines, and built her ports and railways while Irish harbours silted up and Irish factories closed down. While England grew fat on the crops and beef of Ireland, Ireland starved in her own green fields and Irishmen grew lean in the strife of Europe.

While a million Irishmen died of hunger on the most fertile plains of Europe, English Imperialism drew over one thousand million pounds sterling for investment in a world policy from an island that was represented to that world as too poor to even bury its dead. The profit to England from Irish peonage cannot be assessed in terms of trade, or finance, or taxation. It far transcends Lord MacDonnell's recent estimate at Belfast of £320,000,000 – "an Empire's ransom," as he bluntly put it.

....

2   This time-honoured British precept that foreigners should not see for themselves the workings of English rule in Ireland finds frequent expression in the Irish State Papers. In a letter from Dublin Castle of August, 1572, from the Lord Deputy Fitzwilliam to Burghley Elizabeth's chief Minister, we are told that the "three German Earls" with "their conductor," Mr. Rogers, have arrived. The Viceroy adds, as his successors have done up to the present day: "According to Your Lordship's direction they shall travell as little way into the cuntry as I can."

Not an Empire's ransom but the sum of an Empire's achievement, the cost of an Empire's founding, and to-day the chief bond of an Empire's existence. Detach Ireland from the map of the British Empire and restore it to the map of Europe and that day England resumes her native proportions and Europe assumes its rightful stature in the empire of the world. Ireland can only be restored to the current of European life, from which she has so long been purposely withheld by the act of Europe. What Napoleon perceived too late may yet be the purpose and achievement of a congress of nations. Ireland, I submit, is necessary to Europe, is essential to Europe, to-day she is retained against Europe, by a combination of elements hostile to Europe and opposed to European influence in the world. Her strategic importance is a factor of supreme weight to Europe and is to-day used in the scales against Europe.

Ireland is appropriated and used, not to the service of European interests but to the extension of anti-European interests. The *arbitium mundi* claimed and most certainly exercised by England is maintained by the British fleet, and until that power is effectively challenged and held in check it is idle to talk of European influence outside of certain narrow continental limits.

The power of the British fleet can never be permanently restrained until Ireland is restored to Europe. Germany has of necessity become the champion of European interests as opposed to the world domination of England and English-speaking elements. She is to-day a dam, a great reservoir rapidly filling with human life that must some day find an outlet. England instead of wisely digging channels for the overflow has hardened her heart, like Pharaoh, and thinks to prevent it or to so divert the stream that it shall be lost and drunk up in the thirsty sands of an ever expanding Anglo-Saxondom. German laws, German language, German civilization are to find no ground for replenishing, no soil to fertilize and make rich.

I believe this to be not only the set policy of England, but to be based on the temperamental foundations of the English character itself, from which that people could not, even if they would, depart. The lists are set. The English mind, the English consciousness are such, that to oppose German influence in the world is to this people a necessity. They oppose by instinct, against argument, in the face of reason, they will do it blindly come what may and at all costs, and they will do it to the end.

Their reasoning, if reason exists in what is after all a matter of primal instinct, might find expression somewhat as follows:

"German influence cannot but be hostile to British interests. The two peoples are too much alike. The qualities that have made England great they possess in a still greater degree. Given a fair field and no favour they are bound to beat us. They will beat us out of every market in the world, and we shall be reduced ultimately to a position like that of France to-day. Better fight while we are still die stronger. Better hinder now ere it be too late. We have bottled up before and destroyed our adversaries by delay, by money, by alliances. To tolerate a German rivalry is to found a German empire and to destroy our own."

Some such obscure argument as this controls the Englishman's reasoning when he faces the growing magnitude of the Teutonic people. A bitter resentment, with fear at the bottom, a hurried clanging of bolt and rivet in the belt of a new warship and a muffled but most diligent hammering at the rivets of an ever building American Alliance – the real Dreadnought this, whose keel was laid sixteen years ago and whose slow, secret construction has cost the silent swallowing of many a cherished British boast.

English Liberalism might desire a different sort of reckoning with Germany, but English Liberalism is itself a product of the English temperament, and however it may sigh, by individuals, for a better understanding between the two peoples, in the mass, it is a part of the national purpose and a phase of the national mind and is driven relentlessly to the rivets and the hammering, the "Dreadnoughts" in being and that mightier Dreadnought yet to be, the Anglo-Saxon Alliance which Germany must fight if she is to get out.

Doubtless she has already a naval policy and the plans for a naval war, for the fight will be settled on the sea, but the fate will be determined on an island.

The Empire that has grown from an island and spread with the winds and the waves to the uttermost shores will fight and be fought for on the water and will be ended where it began, on an island.

That island, I believe, will be Ireland and not Great Britain.

Chapter III

The Balance of Power

A conflict between England and Germany exists already, a conflict of aims.

England rich, prosperous, with all that she can possibly assimilate already in her hands, desires peace on present conditions of world power. These conditions are not merely that her actual possessions should remain intact, but that no other Great Power shall, by acquiring colonies and spreading its people and institutions into neighbouring regions, thereby possibly affect the fuller development of those pre-existing British States. For, with England equality is an offence and the Power that arrives at a degree of success approximating to her own and one capable of being expanded into conditions of fair rivalry, has already committed the unpardonable sin. As Curran put it in his defence of Hamilton Rowan in 1797, "England is marked by a natural avarice of freedom which she is studious to engross and accumulate, but most unwilling to impart; whether from any necessity of her policy or from her weakness, or from her pride, I will not presume to say."

Thus while England might even be the attacking party, and in all probability will be the attacking party, she will embark on a war with Germany at an initial disadvantage. She will be on her defence. Although, probably, the military aggressor from reasons of strategy, she will be acting in obedience to an economic policy of defence and not of attack. Her chief concern will be not to advance and seize, always in war the more inspiring task, but to retain and hold. At best she could come out of the war with no new gain, with nothing added worth having to what she held on entering it. Victory would mean for her only that she had secured a further spell of quiet in which to consolidate her strength and enjoy the good things already won.

Germany will fight with far other purpose and one that must inspire a far more vigorous effort; she will fight, not merely to keep what she already has, but to escape from an intolerable position of inferiority she knows to be unmerited and forced not by the moral or intellectual superiority of her adversary or due to her own short comings, but maintained by reason of that adversary's geographical position and early seizure of the various points of advantage.

Her effort will be not merely military, it will be an intellectual assertion, a fight in very truth for that larger freedom, that citizenship of the world England is studious to "engross and accumulate" for herself alone and to deny to all others. Thus, while English attack at the best will be actuated by no loftier feeling than that of a man who, dwelling in a very comfortable house with an agreeable prospect resists an encroachment on his outlook from the building operations of his less well lodged neighbour, Germany will be fighting not only to get out of doors into the open air and sunshine, but to build a loftier and larger dwelling, fit tenement for a numerous and growing offspring.

Whatever the structure Germany seeks to erect England objects to the plan and hangs out her war sign "Ancient Lights."

Who can doubt that the greater patriotism and stronger purpose must inspire the man who fights for light, air, and freedom, the right to walk abroad, to learn, to teach, aye, and to inspire others, rather than him whose chief concern it is to see that no one but himself enjoys these opportunities. The means, moreover, that each combatant will bring to the conflict are, in the end, on the side of Germany. Much the same disproportion of resources exists as lay between Rome and Carthage.

England relies on money. Germany on men. And just as Roman men beat Carthaginian mercenaries, so must German manhood, in the end, triumph over British finance. Just as Carthage in the hours of final shock, placing her gold where Romans put their gods, and never with a soul above her ships, fell before the people of United Italy, so shall the mightier Carthage of the North Seas, in spite of trade, shipping, colonies, the power of the purse and the hired valour of the foreign (Irish, Indian, African), go down before the men of United Germany.

But if the military triumph of Germany seems thus likely, the ultimate assurance, nay even the ultimate safety of German civilization can only be secured by a statemanship which shall not repeat the mistake of Louis XIV and Napoleon. The military defeat of England by Germany is a wholly possible achievement of arms, *if the conflict be between these two alone*, but to realize the economic and political fruits of that victory, Ireland must be detached from the British Empire. To leave a defeated England still in the full possession of Ireland would be, not to settle the question of German rights at sea or in world affairs, but merely to postpone the settlement to a second and possibly far greater encounter. It would be somewhat as if Rome, after the first Punic war had left Sicily to Carthage. But Ireland is far more vital to England than Sicily was to Carthage, and is of far more account to the future of Europe on the ocean than the possession of Sicily was to the future of the Mediterranean.

If Germany is to permanently profit from a victory over England, she must free the narrow seas, not only by the defeat of British fleets in being, but by ensuring that those seas shall not again be closed by British fleets yet to be. The German gateway to a free Atlantic can only be kept open through a free Ireland. For just as the English Channel under the existing arrangement, whereby Ireland lies hidden from the rest of Europe, can be closed at will by England, so with Ireland no longer tied to the girdle of England, that channel cannot be locked. The key to the freedom of European navigation lies at Berehaven and not at Dover. With Berehaven won from English hands, England might close the Channel in truth, but Ireland could shut the Atlantic. As Richard Dox put it in 1689, quaintly but truly, in his dedication to King William III, and Queen Mary of his "History of Ireland from the Earliest Times."

> "But no cost can be too great where the prize is of such value, and whoever considers the situation, ports, plenty and other advantages of Ireland will confess that it must be retained at what rate soever; because if it should come into an enemy's hands, England would find it impossible to *flourish* and perhaps difficult to *subsist* without it. To demonstrate this assertion it is enough to say that Ireland lies in the Line of Trade and that all the English vessels that sail to the East, West, and South must, as it were, run the gauntlet between the harbours of Brest and Baltimore; and I might add that the Irish Wool being transported would soon ruin the English Clothing Manufacture. Hence it is that all Your Majesty's Predecessors have kept close to this fundamental maxim of retaining Ireland inseparably united to the Crown of England."

The sole and exclusive appropriation of Ireland and of all her resources has indeed formed, since the Recorder of Kinsale wrote, the mainstay and chief support of British greatness.

The natural position of Ireland lying "in the line of trade," was possibly its chief value, but that "Irish Wool" which was by no means to be allowed free access to world markets typifies much else that Ireland has been relentlessly forced to contribute to her neighbour's growth and sole profit.

I read but yesterday "Few people realise that the trade of Ireland with Great Britain is equal to that of our trade with India, is 13,000,000 pounds greater than our trade with Germany, and 40,000,000 pounds greater than the whole of our trade with the United States." How completely England has laid hands on all Irish resources is made clear from a recent publication that Mr. Chamberlain's "Tariff Commission" issued towards the end of 1912.

This document, entitled "The Economic Position of Ireland and its relation to Tariff Reform," constitutes, in fact, a manifesto calling for the release of Ireland from the exclusive grip of Great Britain. Thus, for instance, in the section "External Trade of Ireland," we learn that Ireland exported in 1910, £63,400,000 worth of Irish produce. Of this Great Britain took £52,600,000 worth, while some £10,800,000 went either to foreign countries, or to British colonies, over £4,000,000 going to the United States. Of these eleven million pounds worth of Irish produce sent to distant countries, only £700,000 was shipped direct from Irish ports.

The remainder, more than £10,000,000, although the market it was seeking lay chiefly to the West, had to be shipped East into and to pay a heavy transit toll to that country for discharge, handling, agency, commission, and reloading on British vessels in British ports to steam back past the shores of Ireland it had just left. While Ireland, indeed, lies in the "line of trade," between all Northern Europe and the great world markets, she has been robbed of her trade and artificially deprived of the very position assigned to her by nature in the great tides of commercial intercourse. It is not only the geographical situation and the trade and wealth of Ireland that England has laid hands on for her own aggrandizement, but she has also appropriated to her own ends the physical manhood of the island. Just as the commerce has been forcibly annexed and diverted from its natural trend, so the youth of Ireland has been fraudulently appropriated and diverted from the defence of their own land to the extension of the power and wealth of the realm that impoverished it at home. The physical qualities of the Irish were no less valuable than "Irish wool" to Empire building, provided always they were not displayed in Ireland.

So long ago as 1613 we find a candid admission in the State papers that the Irish were the better men in the field. "The next rebellion whenever it shall happen, doth threaten more danger to the State than any heretofore, when the cities and walled towns were always faithful; (1) because they have the same bodies they ever had and therein they had and have advantage of us; (2) from infancy they have been and are exercised in the use of arms; (3) the realm by reason of the long peace was never so full of youths; (4) that they are better soldiers than heretofore, their continental employment in wars abroad assures us, and they do conceive that their men are better than ours."

This testimony to Irish superiority, coming as it does from English official sources just three hundred years ago, would be convincing enough did it stand alone. But it is again and again reaffirmed by English commanders themselves as the reason for their failure in some particular enterprise. In all else they were superior to the Irish; in arms, armaments, munitions, supplies of food and money, here the long purse, settled organization and greater commerce of England, gave her an overwhelming advantage. Moreover the English lacked the moral restraints that imposed so severe a handicap on the Irish in their resistance. They owned no scruple of conscience in committing any crime that served their purpose. Beaten often in open fight by the hardier bodies, stouter arms and greater courage of the Irishmen, they nevertheless won the game by recourse to means that no Irishman, save he who had joined them for purposes of revenge or in pursuit of selfish personal aims, could possibly have adopted. The fight from the first was an unequal one. Irish valour, chivalry, and personal strength were matched against wealth, treachery and cunning. The Irish better bodies were overcome by the worse hearts. As Curran put it in 1817 — "The triumph of England over Ireland is the triumph of guilt over innocence."

The Earl of Essex who came to Ireland in 1599 with one of the largest forces of English troops that, up to then, had ever been dispatched into Ireland (18,000 men), had ascribed his complete failure, in writing to the Queen, to the physical superiority of the Irish:

> "These rebels are more in number than your Majesty's army and have (though I do unwillingly confess it), better bodies, and perfecter use of their arms, than those men who your Majesty sends over."

The Queen, who followed the war in Ireland with a swelling wrath on each defeat, and a growing fear that the Spaniards would keep their promise to land aid to the Irish princes, O'Neill and O'Donnell, issued "instructions" and a set of "ordinances" for the conduct of the war in Ireland, which, while enjoining recourse to the usual methods outside the field of battle – (i.e. starvation, "politic courses," assassination of leaders; and the sowing of dissension by means of bribery and promises), required for the conflict, that her weaker soldiers should be protected against the onslaught of the unarmoured Irishmen by head pieces of steel. She ordered "every soldier to be enforced to wear a murrion, because the enemy is encouraged by the advantage of arms to *come to the sword* wherein he commonly prevaileth."

One of the generals of the Spanish King, Philip III, who came to Ireland in the winter of 1601 with a handful of Spanish troops (200 men), to reinforce the small expedition of de Aguila in Kinsale, thus reported on the physical qualities of the Irish in a document that still lies in Salamanca in the archives of the old Irish College. it was written by Don Pedro De Zubiarr on the 16th of January, 1602, on his return to the Asturias. Speaking of the prospect of the campaign, he wrote: "If we had brought arms for 10,000 men we could have had them, for they are very eager to carry on the war against the English. The Irish are very strong and well shaped, accustomed to endure hunger and toil, and very courageous in fight."

Perhaps the most vivid testimony to the innate superiority of the Irishman as a soldier is given in a typically Irish challenge issued in the war of 1641. The document has a lasting interest for it displays not only the "better body" of the Irishman of that day, but something of his better heart as well, that still remains to us.

One Parsons, an English settler in Ireland, had written to a friend to say that, among other things, the head of the Colonel of an Irish regiment then in the field against the English, would not be allowed to stick long on its shoulders. The letter was intercepted by the very regiment itself, and a captain in it, Felim O'Molloy, wrote back to Parsons:

> "I will do this if you please: I will pick out sixty men and fight against one hundred of your choice men if you do but pitch your camp one mile out of your town, and then if you have the victory, you may threaten my Colonel; otherwise, do not reckon your chickens before they are hatched."

The Anglo-Saxon preferred "politic courses" to accepting the Irish soldier's challenge, even where all the advantage was conceded by the Irishman to his foe and all the risks, save that of treachery (a very necessary precaution in dealing with the English in Ireland), cheerfully accepted by the Celt.

This advantage of the "better bodies" the Irish retained beyond all question up to the Famine. It was upon it alone that the Wexford peasantry relied in 1798, and with and by it alone that they again and again, armed with but pike and scythe swept disciplined regiments of English mercenaries in headlong rout from the field.

This physical superiority of his countrymen was frequently referred to by O'Connell as one of the forces he relied on. With the decay of all things Irish that has followed the Famine, these physical attributes have declined along with so much else that was typical of the nation and the man.

It could not to-day be fearlessly affirmed that sixty Irishmen were more than a match for one hundred Englishmen; yet depleted as it is by the emigration of its strongest and healthiest children, by growing sickness and a changed and deteriorated diet the Irish race still presents a type, superior physically, intellectually and morally to the English. It was on Irish soldiers that the English chiefly relied in the Boer War, and it is no exaggeration to say that could all the Irishmen in the ranks of the British army have been withdrawn, a purely British force would have failed to end the war and the Dutch would have remained masters of the field in South Africa.

It was the inglorious part of Ireland to be linked with those "methods of barbarism" she herself knew only too well, in extinguishing the independence of a people who were attacked by the same enemy and sacrificed to the same greed that had destroyed her own freedom.

Unhappy, indeed, is it for mankind, as for her own fate and honour that Ireland should be forced by dire stress of fortune to aid her imperial wrecker in wrecking the fortune and freedom of brave men elsewhere.

That these physical qualities of Irishmen, even with a population now only one tenth that of Great Britain are still of value to the empire, Mr. Churchill's speech on the Home Rule Bill made frankly clear (February, 1913). We now learn that the First Lord of the Admiralty has decided to establish a new training squadron, "with a base at Queenstown," where it is hoped to induce with the bribe of "self-government" the youth of Cork and Munster to again man the British fleet as they did in the days of Nelson, and we are even told that the prospects of brisk recruiting are "politically favourable."

Carthage got her soldiers from Spain, her seamen, her slingers from the Balearic Islands and the coasts of Africa, her money from the trade of the world. Rome beat her, but she did not leave a defeated Carthage to still levy toll of men and mind on those external sources of supply.

Germany must fight, not merely to defeat the British fleet of to-day, but to neutralize the British fleet of to-morrow. Leave Ireland to Great Britain and that can never be. Neutralize Ireland and it is already accomplished.

One of the conditions of peace, and *for this reason* the most important condition of peace that a victorious Germany must impose upon her defeated antagonist is that Ireland shall be separated and erected into an independent European State under international guarantees. England, obviously would resist such conditions to the last, but then the last has already come before England would consent to any peace save on terms she dictated.

A defeated England is a starved England. She would have to accept whatever terms Germany imposed unless those terms provoked external intervention on behalf of the defeated power.

The prize Germany seeks to win from victory is not immediate territorial aggrandizement obtained from annexing British possessions, not a heavy money indemnity wrung from British finance and trade (although this she might have), but German freedom throughout the world on equal terms with Britain. This is a prize worth fighting for, for once gained the rest follows as a matter of course.

German civilization released from the restricted confines and unequal position in which Britain had sought to pen it must, of itself win its way to the front, and of necessity acquire those favoured spots necessary to its wide development. "This is the meaning of his (the German's) will for power; safety from interference with his individual and national development. Only one thing is left to the nations that do not want to be left behind in the peaceful rivalry of human progress that is to become the equals of Germany in untiring industry, in scientific thoroughness, in sense of duty, in patient persistence, in intelligent, voluntary submission to organization." *(History of German Civilization, by Ernst Richard, Columbia University, New York.)*

Once she had reduced Great Britain to an opposition based on peaceful rivalry in human progress, Germany would find the path of success hers to tread on more than equal terms, and many fields of expansion now closed would readily open to German enterprise without that people incurring and inflicting the loss and injury that an attempted invasion of the great self-governing dominions would so needlessly involve. Most of the British self-governing colonies are to-day great States, well able to defend themselves from overseas attack. The defeat of the British navy would make scarcely at all easier the landing of German troops in, say, Australia, South Africa or New Zealand. A war of conquest of those far-distant regions would be, for Germany, an impossible and a stupidly impossible task.

A defeated England could not cede any of these British possessions as a price of peace, for they are inhabited by free men who, however they might deplore a German occupation of London, could in no wise be transferred by any pact or treaty made by others, to other rule than that of themselves. Therefore, to obtain those British dominions, Germany would have to defeat not only England, but after that to begin a fresh war, or a series of fresh wars, at the ends of the earth, with exhausted resources and probably a crippled fleet.

The thing does not bear inspection and may be dismissed from our calculation.

The only territories that England could cede by her own act to a victorious power are such as, in themselves, are not suited to colonization by a white race. Doubtless, Germany would seek compensation for the expense of the war in requiring the transfer of some of these latter territories of the British Crown to herself. There are points in tropical Africa, in the East, islands in the ocean to-day flying the British flag that might, with profit to German trade and influence, be acquired by a victorious Germany. But none of these things in itself, not all of them put together, would meet the requirements of the German case, or ensure to Germany that future tranquil expansion and peaceful rivalry the war had been fought to secure. England would be weakened, and to some extent impoverished by a war ending with such results; but her great asset, her possession beyond price would still be hers – her geographical position. Deprive her to-day, say of the Gold Coast, the Niger, Gibraltar, even of Egypt, impose a heavy indemnity, and while Germany would barely have recouped herself for the out-of-pocket losses of the war, England in fact would have lost nothing, and ten years hence the Teuton would look out again upon the same prospect, a Europe still dominated beyond the seas by the Western islanders.

The work would have to be done all over again. A second Punic war would have to be fought with this disadvantage that the Atlantic Sicily would be held and used still against the Northern Rome, by the Atlantic Carthage.

A victorious Germany, in addition to such terms as she may find it well to impose in her own immediate financial or territorial interests, must so draft her peace conditions as to preclude her great antagonist from ever again seriously imperilling the freedom of the seas. I know of no way save one to make sure the open seas. Ireland, in the name of Europe, and in the exercise of European right to free the seas from the over-lordship of one European island, must be resolutely withdrawn from British custody. A second Berlin Conference, an international Congress must debate, and clearly would debate, with growing unanimity the German proposal to restore Ireland to Europe.

The arguments in favour of that proposal would soon become so clear from the general European standpoint, that save England and her defeated allies, no power would oppose it.

Considerations of expediency no less than naval, mercantile, and moral claims would range themselves on the side of Germany and a free Ireland. For a free Ireland, not owned and exploited by England, but appertaining to Europe at large, its ports available in a sense they never can be while under British control for purposes of general navigation and overseas intercourse, would soon become of such first-rank importance in continental affairs as to leave men stupified by the thought that for five hundred years they had allowed one sole member of their community the exclusive use and selfish misappropriation of this, the most favoured of European islands.

Ireland would be freed, not because she deserved or asked for freedom, not because English rule has been a tyranny, a moral failure, a stupidity and sin against the light; not because Germany cared for Ireland, but because her withdrawal from English control appeared to be a very necessary step in international welfare and one very needful to the progress of German and European expansion.

An Ireland released from the jail in which England had confined her would soon become a populous State of possibly 10,000,000 to 12,000,000 people, a commercial asset of Europe in the Atlantic of the utmost general value, one holding an unique position between the Old and New Worlds, and possibly an intellectual and moral asset of no mean importance. This, and more, a sovereign Ireland means to Europe. Above all it means security of transit, equalizing of opportunity, freedom of the seas – an assurance that the great waterways of the ocean should no longer be at the absolute mercy of one member of the European family, and that one the least interested in general European welfare.

The stronger a free Ireland grew the surer would be the guarantee that the rôle of England "consciously assumed for many years past, to be an absolute and wholly arbitrary judge of war and peace" had gone for ever, and that at last the "balance of power" was kept by fair weight and fair measure and not with loaded scales.

Chapter IV

The Enemy of Peace

I believe England to be the enemy of European peace, and that until her "mastery of the sea" is overmastered by Europe, there can be no peace upon earth or goodwill among men. Her claim to rule the seas, and the consequences, direct and indirect, that flow from its assertion are the chief factors of international discord that now threaten the peace of the world.

In order to maintain that indefensible claim she is driven to aggression and intrigue in every quarter of the globe; to setting otherwise friendly peoples by the ears; to forming "alliances" and ententes, to dissolving friendships, the aim always being the old one, *divide et impera*.

The fact that Europe to-day is divided into armed camps is mainly due to English effort to retain that mastery of the sea. It is generally assumed, and the idea is propagated by English agencies, that Europe owes her burden of armaments to the antagonism between France and Germany, to the loss of Alsace-Lorraine by France, and the spirit and hope of a *revanche* thereby engendered. But this antagonism has long ceased to be the chief factor that moulds European armaments.

Were it not for British policy, and the unhealthy hope it proffers France would ere this have resigned herself, as the two provinces have done, to the solution imposed by the war of 1870. It is England and English ambition that beget the state of mind responsible for the enormous growth of armaments that now over-shadows continental civilization. Humanity, hemmed in in Central Europe by a forest of bayonets and debarred all egress to the light of a larger world by a forbidding circle of dreadnoughts, is called to peace conferences and arbitration treaties by the very power whose fundamental maxim of rule ensures war as the normal outlook for every growing nation of the Old World. If Europe would not strangle herself with her own hands she must strangle the sea serpent whose coils enfold her shores.

Inspect the foundation of European armaments where we will, and we shall find that the master builder is he who fashioned the British Empire. It is that empire, its claim to universal right of pre-emption to every zone and region washed by the waves and useful and necessary for the expansion of the white races, and its assertion of a right to control at will all the seas of all the world that drives the peoples of Europe into armed camps. The policy of the Boer War is being tried on a vaster scale against Europe. Just as England beat the Boers by concentration camps and not by arms, by money and not by men, so she seeks to-day to erect an armourplate barrier around the one European people she fears to meet in the field, and to turn all Central Europe into a vast concentration camp. By use of the longest purse she has already carried this barrier well towards completion. One gap remains, and it is to make sure that this opening, too, shall be closed that she now directs all the force of her efforts. Here the longest purse is of less avail, so England draws upon another armoury. She appeals to the longest tongue in history – the longest and something else.

In order to make sure the encompassing of Europe with a girdle of steel it is necessary to circle the United States with a girdle of lies. With America true to the great policy of her great founder, an America, "the friend of all powers but the ally of none," English designs against European civilization must in the end fail. Those plans can succeed only by active American support, and to secure this is now the supreme task and aim of British stealth and skill. Every tool of her diplomacy, polished and unpolished, from the trained envoy to the boy scout and the minor poet has been tried in turn. The pulpit, the bar, the press; the society hostess, the Cabinet Minister and the Cabinet Minister's wife, the ex-Cabinet Minister and the Royal Family itself, and last, but not least, even "Irish nationality" – all have been pilgrims to that shrine; and each has been carefully primed, loaded, well aimed, and then turned full on the weak spots in the armour of republican simplicity. To the success of these resources of panic the falsification of history becomes essential and the vilification of the most peace-loving people of Europe.

The past relations of England with the United States are to be blotted out, and the American people who are by blood so largely Germanic, are to be entrapped into an attitude of suspicion, hostility and resentment against the country and race from whom they have received nothing but good. Germany is represented as the enemy, not to England's indefensible claim to own the seas, but to American ideals on the American continent. Just as the Teuton has become the "enemy of civilization" in the Old World because he alone has power, strength of mind, and force of purpose to seriously dispute the British hegemony of the seas, so he is assiduously represented as the only threat to American hegemony of the New World.

This, the key note of the attack on Germany, is sounded from every corner of the British Empire, wherever the Imperial editor, resting on the labours of the lash he wields against the coloured toilers in mine and camp, directs his eyes from the bent forms of these indentured slaves of dividend to the erect and stalwart frames of the new Goths who threaten the whole framework of Imperial dividend from across the North Sea. From the *Times* to the obscurest news-sheet of the remotest corner of the British Dominions the word has gone forth.

The Monroe Doctrine, palladium of the Anglo-Saxon world empire, is imperilled by German ambitions, and were it not for the British fleet, America would be lost to the Americans. Wherever Englishmen are gathered to-day their journals, appealing possibly to only a handful of readers, assert that the function of the British fleet is to exclude the European States, with Germany at their head, from South America, not because in itself that is a right and worthy end to pursue, but because that continent is earmarked for future exploitation and control by their "kinsmen" of the United States, and they need the support of those "kinsmen" in their battle against Germany.

I need quote but a single utterance from the mass of seditious libels of this character before me to show how widespread is the propaganda of falsehood and how sustained is the effort being made to poison the American mind against the only people in Europe England genuinely fears, and therefore wholeheartedly hates.

The *Natal Mercury* for instance, a paper written for the little town of Durban and appealing to a population of only some 30,000 whites, in a recent issue (March, 1913), devoted a leader to the approaching "Peace Centennial" of 1914, to be held in commemoration of the signing of the Treaty of Ghent, which ended the second war between Great Britain and the American people in 1814.

"After all, blood is thicker than water," quotes the Natal journal with satisfaction, and after pointing out some latter day indications of rapprochement between England and the United States, it goes on to proclaim the chief function of the British navy and the claim thereby established on the goodwill of America.

"We make mention of them because such incidents are likely to repeat themselves more and more frequently in that competition for naval supremacy in Europe which compels the United States to put her own fleets into working order and to join in the work that England has hitherto been obliged to perform unaided.

"It is England that polices the Seven Seas, and America has reaped no small benefits from the *self-imposed task*, an aspect of the matter to which every thoughtful American is alive. There is a real and hearty recognition in the New World of the *silent barrier* that Great Britain has set up to what might become something more than a dream of expansion into South America on the part of *one* potent European State. It is, indeed, hardly too much to say that the maintenance of the Monroe Doctrine is at the present moment almost as fully guaranteed by England as it is by the country that enunciated the policy and is the chief gainer by it. It is a case in which a *silent understanding* is of far greater value than a formal compact that 'would serve as a target for casual discontent on this side or that'."

The article concludes by proclaiming "the precious permanence of an unseen bond" and the lofty and enduring worth of "good faith mutually acknowledged and the ultimate solidarity of mutual interests rightly perceived." "The ultimate solidarity" aimed at by those who direct these world-wide pronouncements is not one of mere sterile friendship between the American and the British peoples. American friendship with England is only worth having when it can be translated by world acts into enmity against Germany.

It might truly be said of the British Empire to-day that where two or three are gathered together, there hatred of Germany shall be in the midst of them. Turn where he will, from the Colonies to England, from England to her fleet, from the seas to the air, the Englishman lives and moves and has his being in an atmosphere not of love but of hatred. And this too, a hatred, fear, and jealousy of a people who have never injured him, who have never warred upon him, and whose sole crime is that they are highly efficient rivals in the peaceful rivalry of commerce, navigation, and science.

We are told, for instance, in one of the popular London magazines for January, 1913, in an article upon the financial grievances of the British navy that were it not for Germany there would be to-day another Spithead. "Across the North Sea is a nation that some fifty years ago was so afraid of the British navy that it panicked itself into building an iron-clad fleet.

"To-day, as the second naval power, its menace is too great for any up-to-date Spithead mutiny to come off. But the pay question was so acute that it is possibly only the Germans and their 'menace' that saved us from the trouble." But while the "patriotism" of the "lower-deck" may have been sufficiently stout to avert this peril, the patriotism of the "quarter-deck" is giving us a specimen of its quality that certainly could not be exhibited in any other country in the world.

Even as I write I read in the "British Review" how Admiral Sir Percy Scott attacks Admiral Lord Charles Beresford, dubs him the "laughing-stock of the fleet," accuses him of publishing in his book *The Betrayal* a series of "deliberate falsehoods," and concludes by saying that the gallant Admiral is "not a seaman."

And it is a fleet commanded by such Admirals as these that is to sweep the German navy from the seas!

During the Crimean war the allied British and French navies distinguished themselves by their signal failure to effect the reduction of such minor fortresses as Sveaborg, Helsingfors, and the fortified lighthouses upon the Gulf of Finland. Their respective Admirals fired their severest broadsides into each other, and the bombardment of the forts was silenced by the smart interchange of nautical civilities between the two flagships. Napoleon III, who sought an explanation of this failure of his fleet, was given a reply that I cannot refrain from recommending to the British Admiralty to-day. "Well, Sire," replied the French diplomatist, who knew the circumstances, "both the Admirals were old women, but ours was at least a lady." If British Admirals cannot put to sea without incurring this risk, they might, at least, take the gunboat woman with them to prescribe the courtesies of naval debate.

That England to-day loves America, no one who goes to the private opinions of Englishmen, instead of to their public utterances, or the interested eulogies of their press, can for a moment believe.

The old dislike is there, the old supercilious contempt for the "Yankee" and all his ways. "God's Englishman" no more loves an American citizen now than in 1846 when he seriously contemplated an invasion of the United States, and the raising of the negro-slave population against his "Anglo-Saxon kinsmen."

To-day, when we hear so much of the Anglo-Saxon Alliance it may be well to revert to that page of history. For it will show us that if a British premier to-day can speak as Mr. Asquith did on December 16th, 1912, in his reference to the late American Ambassador as "a great American and a kinsman," one "sprung from a common race, speaking our own language, sharing with us by birth as by inheritance not a few of our most cherished traditions and participating when he comes here by what I may describe as *his natural right in our domestic interests and celebrations,*" then this new-found kinship takes its birth not in a sense of common race, indeed, but in a very common fear of Germany.

In the year 1846, the British army was engaged in robbing the Irish people of their harvest in order that the work of the famine should be complete and that the then too great population of Ireland should be reduced within the limits "law and order" prescribed, either by starvation or flight to America.

Fleeing in hundreds and thousands from the rule of one who claimed to be their Sovereign, expelled in a multitude exceeding the Moors of Spain, whom a Spanish king shipped across the seas with equal pious intent, the fugitive Irish Nation found friendship, hope, and homes in the great Celtic Republic of the West. All that was denied to them in their own ancient land they found in a new Ireland growing up across the Atlantic.

The hate of England pursued them here and those who dared to give help and shelter. The United States were opening wide their arms to receive the stream of Irish fugitives and were saying very harsh things of England's infamous rule in Ireland. This could not be brooked. England in those days had not invented the Anglo-Saxon theory of mankind, and a united Germany had not then been born to vex the ineptitude of her statesmen or to profit from the shortcomings of her tradesmen.

So the greatest Ministers of Queen Victoria seriously contemplated war with America and naturally looked around for some one else to do the fighting. The Duke of Wellington hoped that France might be played on, just as in a later day a later Minister seeks to play France in a similar rôle against a later adversary.[3]

The Mexicans, too, might be induced to invade the Texan frontier. But a greater infamy than this was seriously planned. Again it is an Irishman who tells the story and shows us how dearly the English loved their trans-Atlantic "kinsmen" when there was no German menace to threaten nearer home.

....
3   *Sir Edward Grey and the Entente Cordiale*

Commissioned in 1913, Irish artist Sarah Purser's portrait of Roger Casement was undertaken during the period when Casement wrote many of the essays later published in *The Crime against Europe*. The essays reflect Casement's transition from decorated British consul into incorrigible Irish rebel. This portrait of Casement is on permanent display in Leinster House.

Casement stands to the left at the back (wearing a straw hat) in this photograph of senior administrators in the Congo Free State. He had arrived in the Congo in 1884, the year of the Berlin Conference, when European diplomats met to negotiate on issues of trade and commerce determining the future of sub-Saharan Africa. The fact that Casement was mixing with the most senior figures in King Leopold II's regime, so soon after his arrival in Africa, made his later condemnation of the colonial system all the more damning.

In 1892 Casement was recruited into the British colonial service as an intelligence officer and made various forays into the interior to map the hinterland of the Niger Delta. In this photograph, he stands on the right of the group gathered in front of the British consular office at Old Calabar. Seated in front of Casement is Sir Claude Macdonald and beside him sits the African explorer and ethnographer, Mary Kingsley.

In 1898, Casement was posted to Portuguese West Africa. His consular demesne extended beyond Angola across the forested expanses of the Congo Free State. Over the next five years (barring a brief period of special duties during the Boer War), he undertook an extensive and rigorous investigation of the colonial government of King Leopold II's regime. His immense labyrinth of paper work endures to this day as an exhaustive dissection of the structure of gender and racially-motivated violence supporting the Anglo-Belgian extractive economy in sub-Saharan Africa.

Soldiers recruited into King Leopold II's *Force Publique*.

Casement's official investigation of the Congo Free State from 1898-1903 coincided with a rising tide of concern reaching throughout the Atlantic region of the gratuitous brutality and new slaveries used to support the extraction of rubber. The earliest witnesses to these horrors were evangelical faith missionaries who started to report on and photograph the widespread evidence of outrages. These two images were originally magic lantern slides projected in prayer halls across Britain as popular support for Congo reform was galvanised.

IN THE RUBBER COILS.
Scene—The Congo "Free" State.

In the first decade of the new century, the tragedy of the Congo was kept permanently before the public. The issue motivated solidarity on a popular level and transcended political divisions. The story was used in Britain to bolster the humanitarian image of British foreign policy after the public relations disaster resulting from the Boer War. The principal engine for improvement was the Congo Reform Association. This organisation was founded in 1904 by Roger Casement and E.D. Morel, with the help of Alice Stopford Green, during a meeting at the Slieve Donard Hotel in County Down. The long correspondence between 'Bulldog' Morel and 'Tiger' Casement is held at the London School of Economics.

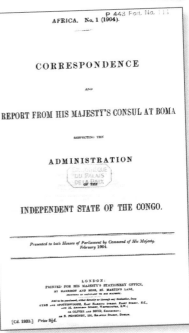

The Irish historian and intellectual, Alice Stopford Green (1848-1929) undertook an investigation of Boer prisoners held in a British POW camp on St Helena in 1900. Soon afterwards she set up the Mary Kingsley Society of West Africa. Her immense network of influential friends proved invaluable to the ultimate success of the Congo Reform Association and to Casement's emergence by 1911 as the moral conscience of the British Empire. Stopford Green was one of four women elected to the first Irish senate. She died on 28 May 1929 in her house at 90 St Stephens Green and was buried in Deans Grange cemetery. This pastel drawing by Sir William Rothenstein is held in the Dublin City Gallery.

E.D. Morel (above) was the tireless acting secretary of the Congo Reform Association. He published a stream of books and pamphlets and organised regular meetings to raise public awareness about the Congo crimes. He found time, too ,to edit the *West African Mail* – a trade paper that carried regular commercial news alongside eye witness accounts of the outrages committed against the communities living in the Congo Free State and other regions of Africa. In 1911, Morel turned his pen against the culture of secrecy within international relations that he rightly forecast was sleepwalking the world towards brutal conflict. This view was similarly reflected in Casement's essays. On the outbreak of war in August 1914, Morel took on the organisational work of the *Union of Democratic Control*.

Edited by EDMUND D. MOREL.

AN ILLUSTRATED WEEKLY JOURNAL founded to meet the rapidly growing interest in West and Central African questions: and representing the commercial, industrial, mining and political interests of West Africa generally.

Of the sixteen leaders executed for their part in the Easter Rising, Roger Casement had the strongest connections to the province of Ulster. After the death of his parents, Casement was raised on the Casement family estate, Magherintemple, in the Glens of Antrim. There he developed a deep love for the landscape and the folkloric tradition of the Glens and made lifelong friendships among the hill farmers and school teachers. In 1904, he participated in the first Feis na nGleann. For the rest of his life, he returned regularly to the Glens to be among his family and friends and expressed a desire to be buried in the spectacular setting of Murlough Bay.

THE SPINNER.

Casement's engagement with the Irish language movement led him into the farthest corners of Ireland. He helped establish initiatives in all four provinces. Here he is pictured (right of centre) with a group of language students at Cloghaneely, County Donegal. Casement was also instrumental in helping to support Bulmer Hobson and Countess Markiewicz in the founding of Fianna na Eireann. In the photograph below, he is seen alongside Alice Stopford Green and members of the Fianna on the steps of Ardrigh, the house of Francis Joseph Bigger in Belfast.

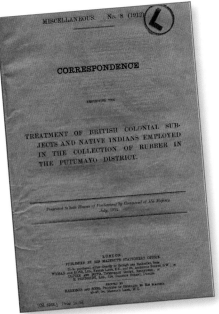

Casement served as British consul in Brazil from 1906-1913. During that posting he carried out an investigation into the abuse of indigenous communities living in the north-west Amazon, victims of the savage extractive rubber industry. His official *Blue Book*, published in 1912, pointed the finger of blame at City of London investors and the systemic failure of international finance to take responsibility for abusive supply chain practices. The heroic story of Casement's investigation was carried in newspapers around the world in the years before the First World War and turned him into a figure of global stature: the moral conscience of the British Empire.

COMMISSION EXPOSES RUBBER HORRORS.

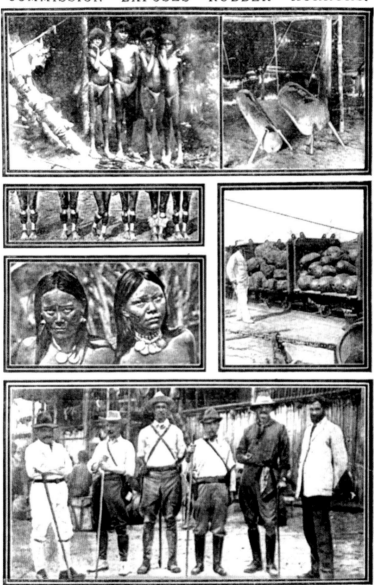

The Daily Mirror, 15 July 1912. Casement is photographed standing with the other commissioners. In 1910, he journeyed with this group into the Putumayo region of the Amazon – a contested frontier region between Brazil, Colombia and Peru – to report on the abusive activities of the British-owned, Peruvian Amazon Company.

Casement was part of a group of Protestant nationalists who organised the running of guns into Howth and Kilcoole at the end of July 1914 to arm the Irish Volunteers. His co-conspirators included Alice Stopford Green, Mary Spring Rice, Erskine & Molly Childers, Sir Thomas Myles and Conor O'Brien. When the guns arrived, Casement was in America raising both funds and the profile of the Irish Volunteers among Irish-American sympathisers and preparing his essays *The Crime against Europe* for publication.

THE·IRISH·VOLUNTEER

☆ ☆ an c-ósláċ ☆ ☆   ★★★

Vol. I. No. 30   Saturday, August 1, 1914   Price 1d.

THE RIGHT TO MURDER!

ENGLAND'S CLAIM.

Ireland's Protest against the Arms Proclamation and England's Answer

The English Government, through the Executive responsible to it, has reasserted its old claim—the right to murder the Irish people without even the formality of a trial.

Bullet and bayonet, rope and poison, were the instruments by which English law was enforced for centuries, and if of late years they were not in use it is not because they were superseded, but because they were held in abeyance for the generation that would question the slaves heritage. Active as instruments or hidden from sight as a menace they were ever ready to fulfil their purpose—to keep the Irish people a race of helots.

Men and women of Ireland—there are stark corpses to-day in Dublin, there are widows and orphans in the streets of Ireland's Capital. Why? Let justice answer if British justice that invests

Casement arrived into Berlin from Norway on 1 November 1914. He would remain in Germany for the next eighteen months. His initially amicable friendship with the German Foreign Office deteriorated as his efforts to recruit an Irish Brigade fell flat among the captured Irish POWs held in the camp at Limburg. In April 1916, Casement boarded a German U-boat with his trusted friend, Captain Robert Monteith, and returned to Ireland with the intention to try and stop the Easter Rising or die beside his comrades. His plan to rendezvous with the arms shipment in Tralee Bay failed. Casement was captured on Good Friday 1916 and spirited out of Ireland on the night ferry from Kingstown (Dún Laoghaire).

Casement's trial for high treason proved to be a deeply political affair. His prosecution was led by his adversary the Attorney General, F.E. "Galloper" Smith. In the background, the instruments of the deep state – Britain's secret intelligence agencies – conspired to orchestrate a vicious and scurrilous smear campaign to destablise Casement's defence and undermine his circles of support. The trial occurred at the end of June and a verdict of guilty was delivered forty-eight hours before the opening explosion of the Battle of the Somme. All pleas for clemency failed. Sir John Lavery was allowed into the jury box during the appeal at the Royal Courts of Justice to capture the moment for posterity. Casement was hanged behind closed doors in Pentonville on 3 August 1916.

THE MOST TIMELY BOOK:

"The Crime Against Europe"

BY

SIR ROGER CASEMENT

The Irish Liberator Condemned to Death

The articles contained in this remarkable little volume (written before the war) expose England's treachery and arrogance towards all nations, against Germany in particular.

Sir Roger points out at the same time the demoralizing influence which England exerts over the United States.

Price 25 Cents

ISSUES AND EVENTS   21 Park Row, New York City

Harry Kernoff's wood cut of *Roger Casement in the Dock* belongs to a long tradition of cultural interventions in the struggle to know the deeper truths about Casement.

Like few other figures from history, Roger Casement's life, death and legacy have intrigued journalists, biographers, novelists, playwrights and public intellectuals for more than a century. Historians have preferred to maintain a state of silence. In 1953, Eamon de Valera made an unauthorised visit to Murlough Bay to inspect veterans of the Antrim brigade of the IRA. In 2017, during a state visit to Peru, President Michael D. Higgins and the Taoiseach-in-waiting, Leo Varadkar visited an exhibition on Roger Casement organised through the co-operation of Ireland and Peru's respective Ministries of Foreign Affairs.

Writing from Carlsruhe, on January 26th, 1846, to his friend, Alexander Spencer, in Dublin, Charles Lever said: "As to the war the Duke[4] says he could smash the Yankees, and ought to do so while France in her present humour and Mexico opens the road to invasion from the South – not to speak of the terrible threat that Napier uttered, that with two regiments of infantry and a field battery he'd *raise the slave population in the United States*."

The infamy of this suggestion cannot be surpassed. The brilliant soldier who conceived it was the chivalrous Englishman who conquered Scinde, one of the chief glories of the Britannic hierarchy of soldier-saints.

The Government planning it was that of the late Queen Victoria with the Duke of Wellington's advice, and the people against whom the black-slave millions were to be loosed were the "kith and kin" of those meditating this atrocious form of massacre. Truly, as an old Irish proverb, old even in the days of Henry VIII. put it, "the pride of France, the *treason of England* and the warre of Ireland shall never have end."

As a latter day witness of that treason, one who had suffered it from birth to the prison cell, a dead Irishman speaks to us from the grave. Michael Davitt in a letter to Morrison Davidson on August 2701, 1902, thus summed up in final words what every Irishman feels in his heart:

> "The idea of being ruled by Englishmen is to me the chief agony of existence. They are a nation without faith, truth or conscience enveloped in a panoplied pharisaism and an incurable hypocrisy. Their moral appetite is fed on falsehood. They profess Christianity and believe only in Mammon. They talk of liberty while ruling India and Ireland against the principles of a constitution, professed as a political faith, but prostituted to the interests of class and landlord rule."

Have Englishmen in less than two generations substituted love for the hate that Napier, Wellington, and the Queen's Ministers felt and expressed in 1846 for the people of the United States? Is it love to-day for America or fear of someone else that impels to the "Arbitration Treaties" and the celebration of the "Hundred years of Peace?"

....

4   The Duke of Wellington: the report was brought to Lever by the Marquis of Douro, the Duke's heir.

The Anglo-American "Peace Movement" was to be but the first stage in an "Anglo-Saxon Alliance," intended to limit and restrict all further world changes, outside of certain prescribed continental limits, to these two peoples alone on the basis of a new "Holy Alliance," whose motto should be *Beati possidentes*.

Since England and America, either in fact or by reservation enjoy almost all the desirable regions of the earth, why not bring about a universal agreement to keep everyone in his right place, to stay "just as we are," and to kindly refer all possible differences to an "International Tribunal?"

Once again the British Bible was thrown into the scale, and the unrighteousness of Germany, who did not see her way to join in the psalm singing, was exposed in a spirit of bitter resignation and castigated with an appropriate selection of texts. The Hague Tribunal would be so much nicer than a war of armaments! With no reckless rivalries and military expenditure there could be no question of the future of mankind.

An idyllic peace would settle down upon the nations, contentedly possessing each in its own share of the good things of life, and no questionable ambitions would be allowed to disturb the buying and selling of the smaller and weaker peoples. The sincerity of the wish for universal arbitration can be best shown by England, when she, or any of the Powers to whom she appeals, will consent to submit the claim of one of the minor peoples she or they hold in subjection to the Hague Tribunal. Let France submit Madagascar and Siam, or her latest victim, Morocco, to the franchise of the Court. Let Russia agree to Poland or Finland seeking the verdict of this bench of appeal. Let England plead her case before the same high moral tribunal and allow Ireland, Egypt, or India to have the law of her. Then, and not until then, the world of little States and beaten peoples may begin to believe that the Peace Crusade has some foundations in honour and honesty but not till then.

Germany has had the straightforwardness and manliness to protest that she is still able to do her own shooting and that what she holds she will keep, by force if need be, and what she wants she will, in her own sure time, take, and by force too, if need be. Of the two cults the latter is the simpler, sincerer, and certainly the less dishonest.

Irish-American linked with German-American keen-sighted hostility did the rest. The rivalry of Mr. Roosevelt and Mr. Taft aided, and the effort (for the time at any rate) has been wrecked, thereby plunging England into a further paroxysm of religious despondency and grave concern for German morals. This mood eventuated in Lord Haldane's "week end" trip to Berlin. The voice was the voice of Jacob, in spite of the hand of Esau. Mr. Churchill at Glasgow, showed the real hand and the mess of pottage so amiably offered at Berlin bought no German birthright. The Kreuz Zeitung rightly summed up the situation by pointing out that "Mr. Churchill's testimony can now be advanced as showing that the will of England alone comes in question as the exponent of peace, and that England for many years past has consciously assumed the rôle of an absolute and perfectly arbitrary judge of war and peace. It seems to us all the more significant that Mr. Churchill proposes also in the future to control, with the help of the strong navies of the Dominions, the trade and naval movements of all the Powers on the face of the earth – that is to say, his aim is to secure a world monopoly for England." There has never been any other thought in the English mind. As I said in Part I. of this paper, "British interests are first the control of all the seas of all the world in full military and commercial control. If this be not challenged peace is permitted; to dispute it seriously means war."

Germany is driven by necessity to dispute it seriously and to overcome it. She cannot get out to play her part in world life, *nay, she cannot hope to ultimately maintain herself at home* until that battle has been fought and won.

Arrangements with England, detentes, understandings, call them what you will, are merely parleys before the fight. The assault must be delivered, the fortress carried, or else Germany, and with her Europe, must resign the mission of the white races and hand over the government and future of the world to one chosen people.

Europe reproduces herself yearly at the present time at the rate of about five million souls. Some three-fifths of the number are to-day absorbed into the life of the Continent, the balance go abroad and principally to North America, to swell the English-speaking world. Germany controls about one-fifth of Europe's natural annual increase, and realising that emigration to-day means only to lose her people and build up her antagonist's strength, she has for years now striven to keep her people within German limits, and hitherto with successful results far in excess of any achieved by other European States. But the limit must be reached, and that before many years are past. Where is Germany to find the suitable region, both on a scale and under conditions of climate, health and soil that a people of say 90,000,000 hemmed in a territory little larger than

France, will find commensurate to their needs? No European people is in such plight.

Russia has the immense and healthy world of Siberia into which to overflow. France, far from needing outlets, increases not at all, and during 1911 showed an excess of close on 40,000 deaths over births. For France the day of greatness is past. A French Empire, in any other sense than the Roman one of commercial and military exploitation of occupied territories and subjugated peoples is gone forever.

France has no blood to give except in war. French blood will not colonize even the Mediterranean littoral. Italy is faced with something of the same problem as Germany, but to a lesser extent. Her surplus population already finds a considerable outlet in Argentina and South Brazil, among peoples, institutions, and language largely approximating to those left behind. While Italy has, indeed need of a world policy as well as Germany, her ability to sustain a great part abroad cannot be compared to that of the Teutonic people. Her claim is not so urgent; her need not so insistent, her might inadequate.

The honesty and integrity of the German mind, the strength of the German intellect, the skill of the German hand and brain, and justice and vigour of German law, the intensity of German culture, science, education and social development, these need a great and healthy field for their beneficial display, and the world needs these things more than it needs the British mastery of the seas. The world of European life needs to-day, as it needed in the days of a decadent Roman Empire, the coming of another Goth, the coming of the Teuton. The interposing island in the North Sea alone intervenes. How to surmount that obstacle, how to win the freedom of the "Seven Seas" for Europe must be the supreme issue for Germany.

If she falls she is doomed to sterility. The supreme test of German genius, of German daring, of German discipline and imagination lies there.

Where Louis XIV., the Directory, and Napoleon failed, will the heirs of Karl the Great see clearly?

And then, when that great hour has struck, will Germany, will Europe, produce the statesman soldier who shall see that the key to ocean freedom lies in that island beyond an island, whose very existence Europe has forgotten?

Till that key is out from the Pirate's girdle, Germany may win a hundred "Austerlitzes" on the Vistula, the Dnieper, the Loire, but until she restores that key to Europe, to paraphrase Pitt, she may "roll up that map of the world; it will not be wanted these fifty years."

Chapter V

The Problem of the Near West

The foregoing reflections and the arguments drawn from them were penned before the outbreak of the war between Turkey and the Balkan Allies.

That war is still undecided as I write (March 1913), but whatever its precise outcome may be, it is clear that the doom of Turkey as a great power is sealed, and that the complications of the Near East will, in future, assume an entirely fresh aspect. Hitherto, there was only the possibility that Germany might find at least a commercial and financial outlet in the Asiatic dominions of the Sultan. There was even the possibility, had Turkey held together, that England, to mitigate pressure elsewhere, would have conceded to an expanding and insistent Germany, a friendly interest and control in Asia Minor. It is true that the greatest possible development, and under the most favoured conditions of German interests in that region, could not have met the needs or satisfied the ever increasing necessities of Teutonic growth; but at least it would have offered a safety valve, and could have involved preoccupations likely to deflect the German vision, for a time, from the true path to greatness, the Western highways of the sea.

An occupation or colonisation of the Near East by the Germanic peoples could never have been a possible solution under any circumstances of the problem that faces German statemanship. As well talk of reviving the Frank Kingdom of Jerusalem.

The occupation by the fair-haired peoples of the Baltic and North Seas of the lands of Turk and Tartar, of Syrian and Jew, of Armenian and Mesopotamian, was never a practical suggestion or one to be seriously contemplated. "East is East and West is West," sings the poet of Empire, and Englishmen cannot complain if the greatest of Western peoples, adopting the singer, should apply the dogma to themselves. Germany, indeed, might have looked for a considerable measure of commercial dominance in the Near East, possibly for a commercial protectorate such as France applies to Tunis and Algeria and hopes to apply to morocco, or such as England imposes on Egypt, and this commercial predominance could have conferred considerable profits on Rhenish industries and benefited Saxon industrialism, but it could never have done more than this. A colonisation of the realms of Bajazet and Saladin by the fair-skinned peoples of the North, or the planting of Teutonic institutions in the valley of Damascus, even with the benevolent neutrality of England, is a far wider dream (and one surely no German statesman ever entertained) than a German challenge to the sea supremacy of England.

The trend of civilized man in all great movements since modern civilization began, has been from East to West, not from West to East. The tide of the peoples moved by some mysterious impulse from the dawn of European expansion has been towards the setting sun. The few movements that have taken place in the contrary direction have but emphasized the universality of this rule, from the days of the overthrow of Rome, if we seek no earlier date. The Crusades furnished, doubtless, the classic example. The later contrary instance, that of Russia towards Siberia, scarcely, if at all affects the argument, for there the Russian overthrow is filling up Northern rather than Eastern lands, and the movement involves to the Russian emigrant no change of climate, soil, law, language or environment while that emigrant himself belongs, perhaps, as much to Asia as to Europe.

But whatever value to German development the possible chances of expansion in the Near East may have offered before the present Balkan war, those chances to-day, as the result of that war, scarcely exist. It is probably the perception of this outcome of the victory of the Slav States that has influenced and accelerated the characteristic change of English public opinion that has accompanied with shouts of derision the dying agonies of the Turk. "In matters of mind," as a recent English writer says in the *Saturday Review*, "the national sporting instinct does not exist. The English public invariably backs the winner." And just as the English public invariably backs the winner, British policy invariably backs the anti-German, or supposedly anti-German side in all world issues. "What 1912 seems to have effected is a vast aggrandizement of the Slavonic races in their secular struggle against the Teutonic races. Even a local and temporary triumph of Austria over Servia cannot conceal the fact that henceforth the way south-east to the Black Sea and the Aegean Sea is barred to the Germans."[5]

....

5   *Mr. Frederick Harrison in the "English Review", January 1913*

That is the outstanding fact that British public opinion perceives with growing pleasure from the break up of Turkey.

No matter where the dispute or what the purpose of conflict may be, the supreme issue for England is "Where is Germany?"

Against that side the whole weight of Great Britain will, openly or covertly, be thrown. German expansion in the Near East has gone by the board, and in its place the development of Greek naval strength in the Mediterranean, to take its stand by the Triple Entente, comes to be jauntily considered, while the solid wedge of a Slav Empire or Federation, commanding in the near future 2,000,000 of armed men is agreeably seen to be driven across South-eastern Europe between Austro-German efforts and the fallow lands of Asia Minor. These latter can safely be left in Turkish hands yet a while longer, until the day comes for their partition into "spheres of influence," just as Persia and parts of China are to-day being apportioned between Russia and England. This happy consummation, moreover, has fallen from heaven, and Turkey is being cut up for the further extension of British interests clearly by the act of God.

The victory of the Balkan States becomes another triumph for the British Bible; it is the victory of righteousness over wrong-doing.

The true virtue of the Balkan "Christians" lies in the possibility of their being moulded into an anti-German factor of great weight in the European conflict, clearly impending, and in their offering a fresh obstacle, it is hoped, to German world policy.

Let us first inspect the moral argument on the lips of these professors. We are assured, by it, that the claim of the Balkan Allies to expel Turkey from Europe rests upon a just and historic basis.

Briefly stated it is that the Turk has held his European provinces by a right of conquest only. What the sword took, die sword may take away. When the sword was struck from the Ottoman's grasp his right to anything it had given him fell too. Thus Adrianople, a city he has held for over five hundred years, must be given up to a new conqueror who never owned it in the past and who certainly has far less moral claim to be there to-day than the descendants of Selim's soldiers.

But the moral argument brings strange revenges.

If Turkey has no right to Adrianople, to Thrace – "right of sword to be shattered by the sword" – what right has England to Ireland, to Dublin, to Cork? She holds Ireland by exactly the same title as that by which Turkey has hitherto held Macedonia, Thrace, Salonika – a right of invasion, of seizure, of demoralization. If Turkey's rights, nearly six hundred years old, can be shattered in a day by one successful campaign, and if the powers of Europe can insist, with justice, that this successful sword shall outweigh the occupation of centuries, then, indeed, have the Powers, led by England, furnished a precedent in the Near East which the victor in the next great struggle should not be slow to apply to the Near West, when a captive Ireland shall be rescued from the hands of a conqueror whose tide is no better, indeed somewhat worse than that of Turkey to Macedonia. And when the day of defeat shall strike for the Turkey of the Near West, then shall an assembled Europe remember the arguments of 1912-13 and a freed Ireland shall be justified on the very grounds England to-day has been the first to advance against a defeated Turkey.

"But the Turk is an Asiatic," say the English Bashaws: to which indeed, Europe might aptly reply, "and are the English European or non-European?" The moral argument, and the "Asiatic argument" are strange texts for the desecrater of Christian Ireland to appeal to against that continent which she would fain hem in with Malayan and Indian battleships, and Canadian and Australasian dreadnoughts. Not the moral argument, but the anti-German argument, furnishes the real ground for the changed British attitude in the present war.

The moral failure of Turkey, her inability to govern her Christian peoples is only the pretext: but just as the moral argument brings its strange revenges and shows an Ireland that has suffered all that Macedonia has suffered, and this at the hands of Christians, and not of Moslems, so the triumph of the Balkan Allies, far from benefiting Britain, must, in the end, react to her detriment.

The present apparent injury to German interests by the closing of South-eastern Europe, and the road to Asia Minor, will inevitably force Germany to still more resolutely face the problem of opening the Western seaways. To think otherwise is to believe that Germany will accept a quite impossible position tamely and without a struggle.

Hemmed in by Russia on the East and the new Southern Slav States on the South-east, with a vengeful France being incited on her Western frontier to fresh dreams of conquest, Germany sees England preparing still mightier armaments to hold and close the seaways of the world. The Canadian naval vote, the Malayan "gift" of a battleship come as fresh rivets in the chain forged for the perpetual binding of the seas, or it might more truly be said, for the perpetual binding of the hands of die German people.

We read in a recent London periodical how these latest naval developments portend the coming of the day when "the Imperial navy shall keep the peace of the seas as a policeman does the peace of the streets. The time is coming when a naval war (except by England), will be as relentlessly suppressed as piracy on the high seas." (*Review of Reviews*, December, 1912.)

The naïve arrogance of this utterance is characteristically English. It is, after all, but the journalistic echo of the Churchill Glasgow speech, and the fullest justification of the criticism of the Kreuz Zeitung already quoted. It does not stand alone; it could be paralleled in the columns of any English paper – Liberal as much as Conservative – every day in the week. Nothing is clearer than that no Englishman can think of other nations save in terms of permanent inferiority. Thus, for instance, in a November (1912) issue of the *Daily News* we find a representative Englishman (Sir R. Edgecumbe), addressing that Liberal journal in words that no one but an Englishman would dream of giving public utterance to. Sir R. Edgecumbe deprecated a statement that had gone round to the effect that the Malayan battleship was not a free gift of the toiling Tamils, Japanese, Chinese, and other rubber workers who make up, with a few Malays, the population of that peninsula, but was really the fruit of an arbitrary tax imposed upon these humble, but indifferent Asiatics by their English administration.

Far from being indifferent, Sir R. Edgecumbe asserted these poor workers nourished a reverence "bordering on veneration" for the Englishman. "This is shown in a curious way by their refusing to call any European 'a white man' save the Englishman alone. The German trader, the Italian and Frenchman all are, in their speech coloured men."

After this appreciation of themselves the English cannot object to the present writer's view that they are non-Europeans.

Thus while the Eastern question is being settled while I write, by the expulsion of the Turk from Europe, England, who leads the cry in the name of Europe, is preparing the exclusion of Europe from all world affairs that can be dominated by sea power. Lands and peoples held for centuries by Turkey by a right not less moral than that by which England has held Ireland, are being forcibly restored to Europe. So be it.

With settlement of the Eastern question by this act of restitution Europe must inevitably gain the clarity of vision to deal with the Western question by a similar act of restoration.

The Western Macedonia must go the way of its Eastern fellow. Like those of the Orient, the problems of the Occident for Europe are twofold – a near Western and a far Western question. Ireland, keeper of the seas, constitutes for Europe the near Western question.

The freedom of those seas and their opening to all European effort alike on equal terms constitutes the far Western question. But in both cases the antagonist of Europe, the non-European power is the same. The challenge of Europe must be to England, and the champion of Europe must be and can be only Germany. No other European people has the power, the strength of mind, of purpose and of arm to accomplish the great act of deliverance. Europe too long blinded to her own vital interests while disunited, must now, under the guidance of a united Germany, resolutely face the problem of freeing the seas.

That war of the seas is inevitable. It may be fought on a continent; it may be waged in the air – it must be settled on the seas and it must mean either the freeing of those seas or the permanent exclusion of Europeans from the affairs of the world. It means for Europe the future, the very existence of European civilization as opposed to the Anglo-Saxon world domination. In that war, Germany will stand not alone as the champion of Europe, she will fight for the freedom of the world.

As an Irishman I have no fear of the result to Ireland of a German triumph. I pray for it; for with the coming of that day the "Irish question" so dear to British politicians, becomes a European, a world question.

With the humbling of Great Britain and the destruction of her sea ownership, European civilization assumes a new stature, and Ireland, oldest and yet youngest of the European peoples, shall enter into free partnership with the civilization, culture, and prosperity that that act of liberation shall bring to mankind.

Chapter VI

The Duty of Christendom

It is only the truth that wounds. An Irishman to-day in dealing with Englishmen is forced, if he speak truly, to wound. That is why so many Irishmen do not speak the truth. The Irishman, whether he be a peasant, a farm labourer, however low in the scale of Anglicization he may have sunk, is still in imagination, if not always in manner, a gentleman. The Englishman is a gentleman by chance, by force of circumstances, by luck of birth, or some rare opportunity of early fellowship. The Irishman is a gentleman by instinct and shrinks from wounding the feelings of another man and particularly of the man who has wounded him. He scorns to take it out of him that way. That is why the task of misgoverning him has been so easy and has come so naturally to the Englishman.

One of the chief grievances of the Irishman in the middle ages was that the man who robbed him was such a boor. Insult was added to injury in that the oppressor was no knight in shining armour, but a very churl of men; to the courteous and cultured Irishman a "bodach Sassenach," a man of low blood, of low cunning, caring only for the things of the body, with no veneration for the things of the spirit with, in fine, no music in his soul. The things that the Irishman loved he could not conceive of. Without tradition or history himself he could not comprehend the passionate attachment of the Irishman to both, and he proceeded to wipe both out, so far as in him lay, from off the map of Ireland and from out the Irishman's consciousness.

Having, as he believed, with some difficulty accomplished his task, he stands to-day amazed at the result. The Irishman has still a grievance – nay more, Ireland talks of "wrongs." But has she not got him? What more can she want except his purse? And, that too, she is now taking. In the indulgence of an agreeable self-conceit which supplies for him the want of imagination he sees Ireland to-day as a species of "sturdy beggar," half mendicant, half pickpocket making off with the proceeds of his hard day's work. The past slips from him as a dream. Has he not for years now, well, for thirty years certainly, a generation, a life time, done all in his power to meet the demands of this incessant country that more in sorrow than in anger he will grant you, was misgoverned in the past. That was its misfortune, never his fault. This is a steadily recurring phase of the fixed hallucination in his blood. Ireland never is, but only always has been cursed by English rule. He himself, the Englishman of the day, is always a simple, bluff, good-hearted fellow. His father if you like, his grandfather very probably, misgoverned Ireland, but never he himself. Why, just look at him now, his hand never out of his pocket relieving the shrill cries of Irish distress. There she stands, a poverty-stricken virago at his door, shaking her bony fist at him, Celtic porter in her eye, the most fearful apparition in history, his charwoman, shaming him before the neighbours and demanding payment for long past spring cleanings that he, good soul, has forgotten all about or is quite certain were settled at the time. Yes, there she stands, the Irish charwoman, the old broom in her hand and preparing for one last sweep that shall make the house sweet and fit for her own children. And John Bull, honest, sturdy John Bull, believing the house to be his, thinks that the only thing between him and the woman is the matter of wages; that all she wants is an extra shilling. Ireland wants but one thing in the world. She wants her house to herself, and the stranger out of her house.

While he is, in his heart, perfectly aware of this, John Bull (for the reasons given by Richard Cox), is quite determined that nothing shall get him out of the house. "Separation is unthinkable," say English Ministers. The task of Ireland is to-day what it always has been to get the stranger out of the house. It is no shame to Ireland or her sons, that up to this they have failed in each attempt. Those attempts are pillars of fire in her history, beacons of light in the desert of sin, where the Irish Israel still wanders in search of the promised land. Few of the peoples in Europe who to-day make up the concert of powers, have, unaided, expelled the invader who held them down, and none has been in the situation of Ireland.

As Mr. Gladstone wrote in 1890, "can anyone say we should have treated Ireland as we have done had she lain not between us and the ocean, but between us and Europe?"

In introducing the scheme of mild Home Rule termed the Councils Bill in 1907, Mr. Birrell prefaced it with the remark that "separation was unthinkable – save in the event of some great world cataclysm." World cataclysms up to this have not reached Ireland – England intervened too well. She has maintained her hold by sea power. The lonely Andromeda saw afar off the rescuing Perseus, a nude figure on the coast of Spain or France, but long ere his flight reached her rock-bound feet she beheld him fall, bruised and mangled, and devoured by the watching sea monster.

Had Italy been placed as Ireland is, cut off from all external succour save across a sea held by a relentless jailor, would she have been to-day a free people, ally of Austria on terms of high equality?

The blood shed by the founders of modern Italy would all have been shed in vain that blood that sanctified the sword of Garibaldi had it not been for the selfish policy of Louis Napoleon and the invading armies of France. Italy, no more than Ireland, could have shaken herself free had it not been for aid from abroad. The late Queen Victoria saw clearly the parallel, and as hereditary custodian of Ireland, Her Majesty protested against the effort then being made to release Italy from an Austrian prison, when she herself was so hard put to it to keep Ireland in an English jail. Writing to her Prime Minister on July 25th, 1848, Her Majesty said:

> "The Queen must tell Lord John (Russell) what she has repeatedly told Lord Palmerston, but without apparent effect, that the establishment of an entente cordiale with the French Republic, for the purpose of driving the Austrians out of their dominions in Italy would be a disgrace to this country. That the French would attach the greatest importance to it and gain the greatest advantage from it, there can be no doubt of. But how will England appear before the world at the moment she is struggling for her supremacy in Ireland?..." and on Oct. 10th following Her Majesty wrote to her uncle, the first King of the Belgians (who owed his new minted crown to the Belgian people depriving the Dutch Sovereign of his "lawful possessions") in the following memorable words:

> "Really it is quite immoral, with Ireland quivering in our grasp, and ready to throw off her allegiance at any moment, for us to force Austria to give up her lawful possessions. What shall we say if Canada, Malta, etc., begin to trouble us? It hurts me terribly." (Page 237, Queen Victoria's letters, published by order of His Majesty, King Edward VII.)

It hurt Ireland much more terribly, that failure to throw off the hand that held her "quivering in our grasp," so soon to stretch her "a corpse upon the dissecting table."

Ireland has failed to win her freedom, not so much because she has failed to shed her blood, but because her situation in the world is just that unique situation I have sought to depict. Belonging to Europe, she has not been of Europe; and England with a persistency that would be admirable were it not so criminal in intention and effect, has bent all her efforts, all her vigour, an unswerving policy, and a pitiless sword to extend the limits of exclusion. To approach Ireland at all since the first English Sovereign laid hands upon it was "quite immoral." When Frederick of Hohenstaufen (so long ago as that!) sent his secretary (an Irishman) to Ireland we read that Henry III of England declared "it hurt him terribly," and ordered all the goings out and comings in of the returned Irish-German statesman to be closely watched.

The dire offence of Hugh O'Neill to Elizabeth was far less his rebellion than his "practises" with Spain. At every cessation of arms during the Nine Years War he waged with England, she sought to obtain from him an abjuration of "foreign aid," chiefly "that of the Spaniard." "Nothing will become the traitor (O'Neill) more than his public confession of any Spanish practices, and his abjuration of any manner of harkening or combining with any foreigners."

Could O'Neill be brought to publicly repudiate help from abroad it would have, the Queen thought, the effect that "in Spain... the hopes of such attempts might be extinguished."

As long as the sea was open to Spain there was grave danger. If Spaniard and Irishman came close together O'Neill's offence was indeed "fit to be made vulgar" all men would see the strength of combination, the weakness of isolation.

> "Send me all the news you receive from Spain for Tyrone doth fill all these parts with strange lies, although some part be true, that there came some munition." It was because O'Neill was a statesman and knew the imperative need to Ireland of keeping in touch with Europe that for Elizabeth he became "the chief traitor of Ireland – a reprobate from God, reserved for the sword."

Spain was to Elizabethan Englishmen what Germany is to-day.

> "I would venture to say one word here to my Irish fellow countrymen of all political persuasions. If they imagine they can stand politically

or economically while Britain falls they are woefully mistaken. The British fleet is their one shield. It if be broken Ireland will go down. They may well throw themselves heartily into the common defence, for no sword can transfix England without the point reaching behind her." (Sir Arthur Conan Doyle, in the *Fortnightly Review*, Feb., 1913, "Great Britain and the Next War.")

The voice is a very old one, and the bogey has done duty for a long time in Ireland. When, to-day, it is from Germany that freedom may be feared, Ireland is warned against the German. When, three hundred years ago the beacon of hope shone on the coast of Spain, it was the Spaniards who were the bad people of history.

Fray Mattheo de Oviedo, who had been sent to Ireland as Archbishop, wrote to King Philip III from O'Neill's stronghold, Dungannon, on June 24, 1600. We might be listening to the voice of the *Fortnightly Review* of yesterday. "The English are making great efforts to bring about a peace, offering excellent terms, and for this purpose the Viceroy sent messengers twice to O'Neill, saying among other things, that Your Majesty is making peace with the Queen, and that his condition will be hopeless. At other times he says that no greater misfortune could happen to the country than to bring Spaniards into it, because they are haughty and vicious and they would destroy and ruin the country." The Irish princes were no fools. "To all this they reply most honourably that they will hold out as long as they have one soldier or there remains a cow to eat."

Hugh O'Neill saw clearly that all compromise between Ireland and England was futile, and that the way of escape was by complete separation and lay only through Europe. He again and again begged the Spanish King to sever Ireland and erect it into an allied State. He offered the crown of Ireland to a Spanish prince, just as three centuries earlier another and a great O'Neill offered the crown of Ireland to Edward Bruce in 1315.

The coming of the Bruce saved Gaelic Ireland for three centuries. Had Philip of Spain sent his son as King to Ireland, her fate had been settled then instead of remaining three centuries later to still confront European statesmanship with an unsolved problem.

In many letters addressed by the Irish leaders to Philip II and Philip III we find the constantly recurring note of warning that to leave England in possession of Ireland meant the downfall of Spain. The Irish princes knew that in fighting England they were in truth fighting the battle of European civilization.

Writing to Philip II from Lifford, on May 16th, 1596, O'Neill and O'Donnell drew the King's attention to the cause of Ireland as the cause of Europe, and in the name of Ireland offered the crown to a Spanish prince. "But inasmuch as we have felt to our great and indescribably harm the evil doings and crimes of those whom the Queen of England is in the habit of sending amongst us, we beg and beseech Your Majesty to send someone well known to you and perfectly fit to be the King of this island, for his own welfare, ours, and that of the Christian State (Christendom)."

They asked for a prince "who will not be unwilling to rule over and live amongst us and to direct and guide our nation, well and wisely." They pointed out how "he will obtain much advantage and glory by so doing," and finally they begged "would that Your Majesty would appoint the Archduke of Austria, now Governor of Flanders, a famous man and worthy of all praise, than whom none would be more acceptable." (The original is in Latin and in the archives of Simancas.)

No more statesmanlike appeal was ever made from Ireland; and had the Archduke of Austria assumed the crown of Ireland in 1596, "now or never" would indeed have become "now and forever." Had Philip II carried out his often repeated promises of sending aid to that country the fate of his own kingdom must have been a very different one.

> "I wish it were possible for me, by word of mouth, to show the importance of this undertaking and the great service that would be rendered thereby to God and His Church, and the great advantage it would be to the service of Your Majesty and the peace of Your States to attack the enemy here."

So wrote in 1600 to Philip II, the Archbishop of Dublin, already quoted, Mattheo de Oviedo.

This prelate had been specially sent to Ireland "to see and understand the state of the country misrepresented by English emissaries at foreign courts."

The wrath of Elizabeth against O'Neill was largely due to his keeping in touch with the continent, whereby the lies of her agents abroad were turned to her own ridicule. To Essex, her Viceroy, she wrote: "Tyrone hath blazed in foreign parts the defeat of regiments, the death of captains, and loss of men of quality in every quarter."

O'Neill not only for years beat her generals in the field, her beat herself and her councillors at their own game. To Essex, in an ecstacy of rage at the loss of the last great army sent, she wrote (September 17th, 1599): "To trust this traitor upon oath is to trust the devil upon his religion. Only this we are sure (for we see it in effect), that you have prospered so ill for us by your warfare, as we cannot but be very jealous lest we should be as well overtaken by the treaty."

(Essex wished to bring O'Neill in by a treaty which, while ostensibly conceding the terms of the Irish prince was to allow the Queen time to carry out her purpose.)

The Irish princes knew Elizabeth and her Ministers, as well as she read Essex. "Believe no news from Ireland of any agreement in this country," they had written to Philip II in 1597, "great offers have been made by the Queen of England, but we will not break our word and promise to your." In a letter written a year earlier (Oct. 18, 1596), replying to the special envoy sent by the king, they said:

> "Since the former envoys left us we have used every means in our power, as we promised we should do, to gain time and procrastination from one day to another. But how could we impose on so clever an enemy so skilled in every kind of cunning and cheating if we did not use much dissimulation, and especially if we did not pretend we were anxious for peace? We will keep firm and unshaken the promises which we made to Your Majesty with our last breath; if we do not we shall incur at once the wrath of God and the contempt of men."

How faithfully they kept those promises and how the Spanish King failed in his, their fate and the bitter ruin of their country shows. That men fighting for Ireland had to meet Elizabeth and her statesmen with something of her own cunning is made very clear to anyone reading the State papers in Ireland. Essex, in one of his "answers" wrote: "I advise Her Majesty to allow me, at my return to Dublin, to conclude this treaty, yielding some of their grants in the present; and when Her Majesty has made secret preparations to enable me to prosecute, I will find quarrels enough to break and give them a deadly blow."

The Irish, however, failed in this contest. They were not sufficiently good liars, and lacked the higher flights of villainy necessary to sustain the encounter. The essential English way in Tudor days, and much later, for administering a deadly blow to an Irish patriot was "assassination." Poison frequently took the place of the knife, and was often administered wrapped in a leaf of the British Bible. A certain Atkinson, knowing the religious nature of Cecil, the Queen's Prime Minister, the founder of a long line of statesmen, foremost as champions of Church and Book, suggested the getting rid of O'Neill by some "poisoned Hosts." This proposal to use the Blessed Sacrament as a veritable Last Supper for the last great Irish chief remains on record, was endorsed by Cecil.

Another Briton, named Annyas, was charged to poison "the most dangerous and open rebel in Munster," Florence MacCarthy More, the great MacCarthy. Elizabeth's Prime Minister piously endorsed the deed "though his soul never had the thought to consent to the poisoning of a dog, much less a Christian ."

To Carew, the President of Munster, Cecil wrote enjoining the assassination of the young Earl of Desmond, then "in the keeping of Carew": "Whatever you do to abridge him out of Providence shall never be imputed to you for a fault, but exceedingly commended by the Queen." After this, we are not surprised to learn that in her instructions to Mountjoy, the successor of Essex, the Queen recommended "to his special care to preserve the true exercise of religion among her loving subjects." As O'Neill was still in the field with a large army, she prudently pointed out, however, that the time "did not permit that he should intermeddle by any severity or violence in matters of religion until her power was better established there to countenance his action." That the character of their adversary was faithfully appreciated by contemporary Irish opinion stands plain in a letter written by James Fitzthomas, nephew of the great Earl Gerald of Desmond, to Philip II. "The government of the English is such as Pharaoh himself never used the like; for they content not themselves with all temporal prosperity, but by cruelty desire our blood and perpetual destruction to blot out the whole remembrance of our posterity for that Nero, in his time, was far inferior to that Queen in cruelty."

The Irish chiefs well sustained their part in meeting this combination of power and perfidy, and merited, on the highest grounds of policy the help so often promised by the King of Spain. They showed him not only by their valour on the field but by their sagacious council how great a part was reserved for Ireland in the affairs of Europe if he would but profit from it and do his part.

In this the Spanish King failed. Philip II had died in 1598, too immersed in religious trials to see that the centre of his griefs was pivoted on the possession of Ireland by the female Nero. With his son and successor communication was maintained and in a letter of Philip III to O'Neill, dated from Madrid, Dec. 24th, 1599, we read: "Noble and well beloved I have already written a joint letter to you and your relative O'Donnell, in which I replied to a letter of both of you. By this, which I now write to you personally I wish to let you know my good will towards you, and I mean to prove it, not only by word, but by deed." That promise was not fulfilled, or so inadequately fulfilled that the help, when it came, was insufficient to meet the needs of the case.

History tells us what the sad consequences were to the cause of civilisation in Ireland, from the failure of the Spanish King to realize the greatness of his responsibilities. But the evil struck deeper than to Ireland alone. Europe lost more than her historians have yet realised from the weakness of purpose that let Ireland go down transfixed by the sword of Elizabeth.

Had the fate of Europe been then controlled by a Hohenzollern, instead of by a Spanish Hapsburg, how different might have been the future of the world!

Although Europe had forgotten Ireland, Ireland had never forgotten Europe. Natural outpost and sentinel of that continent in the West for three-hundred years now gagged and bound, since the flight to Rome of her last native Princes, she stands to-day as in the days of Philip III, if an outcast from European civilization non the less rejecting the insular tradition of England, as she has rejected her insular Church. And now once more in her career she turns to the greatest of European Sovereigns, to win his eyes to the oldest, and certainly the most faithful of European peoples. Ireland already has given and owes much to Germany.

In the dark ages intercourse between the Celtic people of the West and the Rhinelands and Bavaria was close and long sustained. Irish monasteries flourished in the heart of Germany, and German architecture gave its note possibly to some of the fairest cathedral churches in Ireland.

Clonfert and Cashel are, perhaps amongst the most conspicuous examples of the influence of that old-time intercourse with Germany. To-day, when little of her past remains to venerate, her ancient language on what seemed its bed of death owes much of its present day revival to German scholarship and culture. Probably the foremost Gaelic scholar of the day is the occupant of the Chair of Celtic at Berlin University, and Ireland recognises with a gratitude she is not easily able to express, all that her ancient literature owes to the genius and loving intellect of Dr. Kuno Meyer.

The name of Ireland may be known on the Bourses or in the Chancelleries of Europe; it is not without interest, even fame, in the centres of German academical culture. But that the German State may also be interested in the political fate of Ireland is believed by the present writer.

Maurice Fitzgerald, the outlawed claimant to the Earldom of Desmond, wrote to Philip II, from Lisbon on September 4th, 1593:

> "We have thought it right to implore your Majesty to send the aid you will think fit and with it to send us (the Irish refugees in the Peninsula) to defend and uphold the same undertaking; for we hope, with God's help Your Majesty will be victorious and conquer and hold as your own the kingdom of Ireland. We trust in God that Your Majesty and the Council will weigh well the advantages that will ensue to Christendom from this enterprise since the opportunity is so good and the cause so just and weighty, and the undertaking so easily completed."

The history of human freedom is written in letters of blood. It is the law of God. No people who clutch to safety, who shun death are worthy of freedom.

The dead who die for Ireland are the only live men in a free Ireland. The rest are cattle. Freedom is kept alive in man's blood only by shedding of that blood. It was not an act of a foreign Parliament they were seeking, those splendid "scorners of death," the lads and young men of Mayo, who awaited with a fearless joy the advance of the English army fresh from the defeat of Humbert in 1798. Then, if ever, Irishmen might have run from a victorious and pitiless enemy who, having captured the French General and murdered in cold blood the seven hundred Killala peasants who were with his colours, were now come to Killala itself to wreak vengeance on the last stronghold of Irish rebellion.

The ill-led and half armed peasants, the last Irishmen in Ireland to stand the pitched fight for their country's freedom, went to meet the army of England, as the Protestant Bishop, who saw them, says: "running upon death with as little appearance of reflection or concern as if they were hastening to a show."

The late Queen Victoria, in one of her letters to her uncle, the King of the Belgians, wrote thus of the abortive rising of fifty years later in 1848:

"There are ample means of crushing the rebellion in Ireland, and I think it is very likely to go off without any contest, which people (and I think rightly) rather regret. The Irish should receive *a good lesson or they will begin again*." (Page 223, Vol. II, Queen Victoria's letters.)

Her Majesty was profoundly right. Ireland needed that lesson in 1848, as she needs it still more to-day. Had Irishmen died in 1848 as they did in 1798 Ireland would be to-day fifty years nearer to freedom. It is because a century has passed since Europe saw Ireland willing to die that to-day Europe has forgotten that she lives.

As I began this essay with a remark of Charles Lever on Germany so shall end it here with a remark of Lever on his own country, Ireland.

In a letter to a friend in Dublin, he thus put the epitaph of Europe on the grave of a generation who believed that "no human cause was worth the shedding one drop of human blood."

> "As to Ireland all foreign sympathy is over owing to the late cowardice and poltroonery of the patriots. *Even Italians can fight*" (Letter of C. Lever from Florence, August 19th, 1848).

It is only the truth that wounds. It is that reproach that has cursed Ireland for a century.

Sedition, the natural garment for an Irishman to wear, has been for a hundred years a bloodless sedition. It is this fiery shirt of Nessus that has driven our strong men mad. How to shed our blood with honour, how to give our lives for Ireland that has been, that is the problem of Irish nationality.

Chapter VII

The Freedom of the Seas

It would be idle to attempt to forecast the details of a struggle between Great Britain and Germany. That is a task that belongs to the War Department of the two States. I have assigned myself merely to point out that such a struggle is inevitable, and to indicate what I believe to be the supreme factors in the conflict, and how one of these, Ireland, and that undoubtedly the most important factor, has been overlooked by practically every predecessor of Germany in the effort to make good at sea. The Spaniards in Elizabeth's reign, the French of Louis XIV and of the Directory took some steps, it is true, to challenge England's control of Ireland, but instead of concentrating their strength upon that line of attack they were content to dissipate it upon isolated expeditions and never once to push home the assault on the one point that was obviously the key to the enemy's whole position. At any period during that last three centuries, with Ireland gone, England was, if not actually at the mercy of her assailants, certainly reduced to impotency beyond her own shores. But while England knew the value to herself of Ireland, she appreciated to the full the fact that this profitable juxtaposition lay on her right side hidden from the eyes of Europe.

"Will anyone assert," said Gladstone, "that we would have dared to treat Ireland as we have done had she lain, not between us and the ocean, but between us and the continent?" And while the bulk of England, swollen to enormous dimensions by the gains she drew from Ireland interposed between her victim and Europe, her continental adversaries were themselves the victims of that strange mental disease psychologists term the collective illusion. All the world saw that which in fact did not exist. The greatness of England as they beheld it, imposing, powerful, and triumphant, existed not on the rocky base they believed they saw, but on the object, sacked, impoverished, and bled, they never saw. And so it is to-day. The British Empire is the great illusion. Resembling in much the Holy Roman Empire it is not British, it is not an Empire, and assuredly it is not holy. It lives on the life-blood and sufferings of some, on the suffrance and mutual jealousy of others, and on the fixed illusion of all. Rather is it a great Mendicity

Institute. England now, instead of "robbing from Pole to Pole," as John Mitchel once defined her activities, goes begging from Pole to Pole that all and every one shall give her a helping hand to keep the plunder. Chins, Goorkhas, Sikhs, Malays, Irish, Chinese, South African Dutch, Australasians, Maoris, Canadians, Japanese, and finally "Uncle Sam" these are the main components that when skilfully mixed from London, furnish the colouring material for the world-wide canvas. If we take away India, Egypt and the other coloured races the white population that remains is greatly inferior to the population of Germany, and instead of being a compact, indivisible whole, consists of a number of widely scattered and separated communities, each with separate and absorbing problems of its own, and more than one of them British neither in race, speech, nor affection. Moreover if we turn to the coloured races we find that the great mass of the subjects of this Empire have less rights within it than they possess outside its boundaries, and occupy there a lower status than that accorded to most foreigners.

The people of India far out number all other citizens of the British Empire put together, and yet we find the British Indians resident in Canada, to take but one instance, petitioning the Imperial Government in 1910 for as favourable terms of entry into that British possession as the Japanese enjoyed.

They pointed out that a Japanese could enter Canada on showing that he held from six pounds to ten pounds, but that no British Indian could land unless he had forty pounds and had come direct from India, – a physical impossibility, since no direct communication exists. But they went further, for they showed that their "citizenship" of the British Empire entailed penalties that no foreign state anywhere imposed upon them.

"We appeal," they said, "and most forcibly bring to your notice that no such discriminating laws are existing against us in foreign countries like the United States of America, Germany, Japan, and Africa, to whom we do not owe any allegiance whatsoever."

So that outside its white or European races it is clear the Empire has no general or equal citizenship, and that, far from being one, it is more divided racially against itself than are even opposing Asiatic and European nations which have the good fortune not to be united in a common, imperial bond.

The total white population of this incongruous mass in 1911 consisted of some 59,000,000 human beings made up of various national and racial strains, as against 66,000,000 of white men in the German Empire the vast majority of them of German blood. And while the latter form a disciplined, self-contained, and self-supporting and self-defending whole, the former are swelled by Irish, French-Canadians, and Dutch South Africans who, according to Sir R. Edgcumbe, must be reckoned as "coloured."

It is one thing to paint the map red, but you must be sure that your colours are fast and that the stock of paints wont run out. England, apart from her own perplexities is now faced with this prospect. Great Britain can no longer count on Ireland, that most prolific source of supply of her army, navy, and industrial efforts during the last century, while she is faced with a declining birth-rate, due largely, be it noted, to the diminished influx of the Irish, a more prolific and virile race. While her internal powers of reproduction are failing, her ability to keep those already born is diminishing still more rapidly. Emigration threatens to remove the surplus of births over deaths.

As long as it was only the population of Ireland that fell (8,500,000 in 1846 to 4,370,000 in 1911), Great Britain was not merely untroubled but actually rejoiced at a decrease in numbers that made the Irish more manageable, and yet just sufficiently starvable to supply her with a goodly surplus for army, navy, and industrial expansion in Great Britain. Now that the Irish are gone with a vengeance it is being perceived that they did not take their vengeance with them and that the very industrial expansion they built up from their starving bodies and naked limbs contains within itself the seeds of a great retribution.

"Since Free Trade has ruined our agriculture, our army has become composed of starving slum dwellers who, according to the German notion are better at shouting than at fighting. German generals have pointed out that in the South African war our regular and auxiliary troops often raised the white flag and surrendered, without necessity, sometimes to a few Boers, and they may do the same to a German invading force. Free Trade which "benefits the consumer" and the capitalist has, unfortunately, through the destruction of our agriculture and through forcing practically the whole population of Great Britain into the towns, destroyed the manhood of the nation." (*Modern Germany* page 251, by J. Ellis Barker, 1907).

An army of slum dwellers is a poor base on which to build the structure of a perpetual world dominion.

While the navy shows an imposing output of new battleships and cruisers for 1913, the record, we are told, of all warship construction in the world, it takes blood as well as iron to cement empires. Battleships may become so much floating scrap iron (like the Russian fleet at Tsushima), if the men behind the guns lack the right stamina and education.

We learn, too, that it is not only the slum dwellers who are failing, but that to meet the shortage of officers a large number of transfers from the merchant marine to the Royal Navy are being sanctioned. To this must be added the call of the Great Dominions for men and officers to man their local fleets. As the vital resources of England become more and more inadequate to meet the menace of German naval and moral strength, she turns her eyes to Ireland, and we learn from the London *Daily Telegraph* that Mr. Churchill's scheme of recruiting at Queenstown may furnish "matter for congratulation, as Irish boys make excellent bluejackets happy of disposition, amenable to discipline, and extremely quick and handy."

As I can recall an article in this same journal, written during the course of the Boer War, in which Ireland was likened to a "serpent whose head must be crushed beneath the heel," the *Daily Telegraph's* praise to-day of the Irish disposition should leave Irish boys profoundly unmoved and still ashore.

There is yet another aspect of the growing stream of British emigration. "Death removes the feeble, emigration removes the strong. Canada, New Zealand, Australia, and South Africa, have no use for the sick and palsied, or of those incapable of work through age or youth. They want the workers and they get them. Those who have left the United Kingdom during 1912 are not the scum of our islands, but the very pick. And they leave behind, for our politicians to grapple with, a greater proportion of females, of children and of disabled than ever before." (*London Magazine!*)

The excess of females over males, already so noteworthy a feature of England's decay, becomes each year more accentuated and doubtless accounts for the strenuous efforts now being made to entrap Irish boys into the British army and navy.

If we compare the figures of Germany and Great Britain, and then contrast them with those of Ireland, we shall see, at a glance, how low England is sinking, and how vitally necessary it is for her to redress the balance of her own excess of "militants" over males by kidnapping Irish youths into her emasculated services and by fomenting French and Russian enmities against the fruitful German people.

Germany, 1910: males, 32,031,967; females, 32,871,456; total, 64,925,993. Excess of females, 739,489.

Great Britain, 1911: England and Wales – males, 17,448,476; females, 18,626,793; total, 36,075,269. Excess of females, 1,178,317.
Scotland – males, 2,307,603; females, 2,251,842; total, 4,759,445. Excess of females, 144,239.

Total for Great Britain, 40,834,714. Excess of females, 1,322,556.

Thus on a population much less than two thirds that of Germany Great Britain has almost twice as many females in excess over males as Germany has, and this disproportion of sexes tends yearly to increase. We read in every fresh return of emigration that it is men and not women who are leaving England and Scotland. That Irish emigration, appalling as its ravages have been since 1846, is still maintained on a naturally healthier basis the sex returns for 1911 make clear. The figures for Ireland at the census were as follows:

Ireland – males, 2,186,802; females, 2,195,147; total, 4,381,949. Excess of females, 8,346.

Ireland, it is seen, can still spare 100,000 or 150,000 males for the British armed forces and be in no unhealthier sex plight than Scotland or England is in. It is to get this surplus of stout Irish brawn and muscle that Mr. Churchill and the British War Office are now touting in Ireland.
I take the following Government advertisement from the Cork *Evening Echo* (of March, 1913), in illustration:

> "Notice – Any person that brings a recruit for the Regular or Special Reserve Branches of the Army to the Recruiting Officer at Victoria Barracks, Cork, will be paid the money reward allowed for each recruit which ranges from 1/6 to 5/- each."

From whatever point of view we survey it we shall find that England's Empire at bottom rests upon Ireland to make good British deficiencies. The Dominions are far off, and while they may give battleships they take men. Ireland is close at hand – she gives all and takes nothing. Men, mind, food and money – all these she has offered through the centuries, and it is upon these and the unrestricted drain of these four things from that rich mine of human fertility and wealth that the British Empire has been founded and maintained. To secure to-day the goodwill and active co-operation of the Irish race abroad as well as in Ireland, and through that goodwill to secure the alliance and support of the United States has become the guiding purpose of British statesmanship.

The Home Rule Bill of the present Liberal Government is merely the petty party expression of what all English statesmen recognize as a national need. Were the present Liberal Government thrown out to-morrow their Unionist successors would hasten to bind Ireland (and America) to them by a measure that, if necessary, would go much further. Every Unionist knows this. Ireland is always the key to the situation.

I will quote two pronouncements, one English and one American, to show that Home Rule has now become an imperial necessity for England.

Speaking in the House of Lords on the Home Rule Bill, Earl Grey, the late Governor-General of Canada, said on January 27th, 1913:

> "In the interests of the Empire I feel very strongly that it is imperative that the Irish question should be settled on lines which will satisfy the sentiment of the over-sea democracies, both in our self-governing colonies and in the United States. Everyone, I think will agree that it is most important and in the highest interests of the empire that there should be the friendliest feelings of generous affection and goodwill, not only between the self-governing Dominions and the Motherland, but also between America and England.... I need not elaborate this point. We are all agreed upon it. A heavy shadow at present exists, and it arises from our treatment of Ireland.... If this be so is it not our duty to remove the obstacle that prevents that relationship with America from being that which we all desire?"

The American utterance came from one equally representative of American Imperial interests. It is that of Mr. Roosevelt, published in the *Irish World* of New York, Feb. 8th, 1913.

> "I feel that the enactment into law of this measure... bids fair to establish goodwill among the English-speaking peoples. This has been

prevented more than by any other one thing by this unhappy feud that has raged for centuries, and the settlement of which, I most earnestly hope, and believe, will be a powerful contribution to the peace of the world, based on international justice and goodwill. I earnestly feel that the measure is as much in the interests of Great Britain as of Ireland."

Did we judge of Ireland only by many of the public utterances made in her name, then, indeed might we despair of a people who having suffered so much and so valiantly resisted for so many centuries were now to be won to their oppressor's side, by, perhaps, the most barefaced act of bribery ever attempted by a Government against a people.

"Injured nations cannot so entirely forgive their enemies without losing something of their virility, and it grates upon me to hear leader after leader of the Parliamentary Party declaring without shame that Home Rule when it is won for Ireland is to be used for a new weapon of offence in England's hands against the freedom of the world elsewhere."

Did the Irish Parliamentary Party indeed represent Ireland in this, Mr. Wilfred Blunt's noble protest in his recent work, *The Land War in Ireland*, would stand for the contemptuous impeachment, not of a political party but of a nation.

Mr. Redmond in his latest speech shows how truly Mr. Blunt has depicted his party's aim; but to the credit of Ireland it is to be recorded that Mr. Redmond had to choose not Ireland, but England for its delivery. Speaking at St. Patrick's Day dinner in London on March 17th, 1913, Mr. Redmond, to a non-Irish audience, thus hailed the future part his country is to play under the restoration of what he describes as a "National Parliament."

"We will, under Home Rule, devote our attention to education, reform of the Poor Law, and questions of that kind which are purely domestic, which are, if you like, hum-drum Irish questions, and the only way in which we will attempt to interfere in any Imperial question will be by our representatives on the floor of the Imperial Parliament in Westminster doing everything in our power to increase the strength and the glory of what will then be our empire at long last; and by sending in support of the empire the strong arms and brave hearts of Irish soldiers and Irish sailors, to maintain the traditions of Irish valour in every part of the world. That is our ambition."

Were this indeed the ambition of Ireland, did this represent the true feeling of Irishmen towards England, and the Empire of England, then Home Rule, on such terms, would be a curse and a crime. Thierry, the French historian, is a truer exponent of the passionate aspirations of the Irish heart than anyone who to-day would seek to represent Ireland as willing to sell her soul no less than the strong arms and brave hearts of her sons in an unholy cause.

"... For notwithstanding the mixture of races, the intercommunion of every kind brought about by the course of centuries, hatred of the English Government still subsists as a native passion in the mass of the Irish nation. Ever since the hour of invasion this race of men has invariably desired that which their conquerors did not desire, detested that which they liked, and liked that which they detested ... This indomitable persistency, this faculty of preserving through centuries of misery the remembrance of lost liberty, and of never despairing of a cause always defeated, always fatal to those who dared to defend it, is perhaps the strangest and noblest example ever given by any nation." (*Histoire De La Conquete De L'Angleterre Par Les Normands*, Paris edition, 1846. London, 1891.)

The French writer here saw deeper and spoke truer than many who seek to-day not to reveal the Irish heart, whose deep purpose they have forgotten, but barter its life-blood for a concession that could be won to-morrow by half that blood if shed at home, thus offered without warrant "as a new weapon of offence to England's hands against the freedom of the world elsewhere."

The Irishman, who in the belief that Home Rule has come or that any measure of Home Rule the London Parliament will offer can be a substitute for his country's freedom, joins the British army or navy is a voluntary traitor to his country. Almost everything that Ireland produces, or consumes, must all go out or come solely through England and on payment of a transit and shipping tax to English trade.

The London press has lately waxed indignant over Servia denied by Austria a port on the Adriatic, and we have been told a Servia without a port is a Servia held in "economic slavery," and that her independence is illusory unless she have free outlet to the sea. But what of Ireland? With not one, but forty ports, the finest in all Western Europe, they lie idle and empty. With over 1,000 miles of seaboard, facing the West and holding the seaway between Europe and

America, Ireland, in the grip of England, has been reduced to an economic slavery that has no parallel in civilization.

And it is to this island, to this people that the appeal is now made that we should distrust the Germans and aid our enslavers. Better far, were that the only outcome, the fate of Alsace-Lorraine (who got their Home Rule Parliament years ago) than the "friendship" of England. We have survived the open hate, the prolonged enslavement, the secular robbery of England and now the England smiles and offers us with one hand Home Rule to take it away with the other, are we going to forget the experience of our forefathers? A Connacht proverb of the Middle Ages should come back to us – "Three things for a man to avoid; the heels of a horse, the horns of a bull; and the smile of an Englishman."

That Ireland must be involved in any war that Great Britain undertakes goes without saying; but that we should willingly throw ourselves into the fray on the wrong side to avert a British defeat, is the counsel of traitors offered to fools.

We must see to it that what Thierry wrote of our fathers is not shamefully belied by their sons. Our "indomitable persistency" has up to this excelled and subdued the unvarying will applied to one unvarying purpose of those who, by dint of that quality, have elsewhere subjugated the universe. We who have preserved through centuries of misery, the remembrance of lost liberty, are not now going to merge our unconquered souls in the base body of our oppressor.

One of the few Liberal statesmen England has produced, certainly the only Liberal politician she has ever produced, the late Mr. Gladstone, compared the union between Great Britain and Ireland to "the union between the mangled corpse of Hector and the headlong chariot of Achilles." (1890.)

But, while I cannot admit that England is an Achilles, save, perhaps, that she may be wounded like him in the heel, I will not admit, I will not own that Ireland, however mangled, however "the plowers have ploughed upon her back and made long furrows," is in truth dead, is indeed a corpse. No; there is a juster analogy, and one given us by the only Englishman who was in every clime, and in every circumstance a Liberal; one who died fighting in the cause of liberty, even as in life he sang it. Byron denounced the union between England and Ireland as "the union of the shark with its prey."

111

Chapter VIII

Ireland, Germany and the Next War

In the February, 1913, *Fortnightly Review*, Sir Arthur Conan Doyle at the end of an article, "Great Britain and the Next War," thus appeals to Ireland to recognize that her interests are one with those of Great Britain in the eventual defeat of the latter:

> "I would venture to say one word here to my Irish fellow-countrymen of all political persuasions. If they imagine that they can stand politically or economically while Britain falls they are woefully mistaken. The British fleet is their one shield. If it be broken Ireland will go down. They may well throw themselves heartily into the common defence, for no sword can transfix England without the point reaching Ireland behind her...."

I propose to briefly show that Ireland, far from sharing the calamities that must necessarily fall on Great Britain from defeat by a great power, might conceivably thereby emerge into a position of much prosperity.

I will agree with Sir A. Conan Doyle up to this – that the defeat of Great Britain by Germany must be the cause of a momentous change to Ireland: but I differ from him in believing that that change must necessarily be disastrous to Ireland. On the contrary, I believe that the defeat of Great Britain by Germany might conceivably (save in one possible condition) result in great gain to Ireland.

The conclusion that Ireland must suffer all the disasters and eventual losses defeat would entail on Great Britain is based on what may be termed the fundamental maxim that has governed British dealings with Ireland throughout at least three centuries. That maxim may be given in the phrase, "Separation is unthinkable." Englishmen have come to invincibly believe that no matter what they may do or what may betide them, Ireland must inseparably be theirs, linked to them as surely as Wales or Scotland, and forming an eternal and integral part of a whole whose fate is indissolubly in their hands. While Great Britain, they admit, might well live apart (and happily) from an Ireland safely "sunk under the sea" they have never conceived of an Ireland, still afloat, that could possibly exist, apart from Great Britain. Sometimes, as a sort of bogey, they hold out to Ireland the fate that would be hers if, England defeated, somebody else should "take" her. For it is a necessary corollary to the fundamental maxim already stated, that Ireland, if not owned by England, must necessarily be "owned" by someone else than her own inhabitants.

The British view of the fate of Ireland in the event of British defeat may be stated as twofold. Either Ireland would remain after the war as she is to-day, tied to Great Britain, or she *might* be (this is not very seriously entertained) annexed by the victor. No other solution, I think, has ever been suggested. Let us first discuss No. I.

This, the ordinary man in the street view, is that as Ireland would be as much a part and belonging to Great Britain after a war as before it, whatever the termination of that war might be, she could not fail to share the losses defeat must bring to a common realm. The partnership being indissoluble, if the credit of the house were damaged and its properties depreciated, all members of the firm must suffer. In this view, an Ireland weaker, poorer, and less recuperative than Great Britain, would stand to lose even more from a British defeat than the predominant partner itself. Let us at once admit that this view is correct. If on the condition of a great war Ireland were still to remain, as she is to-day, an integral portion of a defeated United Kingdom, it is plain she would suffer, and might be made to suffer possibly more even than fell to the share of Great Britain.

But that is not the only ending defeat might bring to the two islands. We must proceed then to discuss No. 2, the alternative fate reserved for Ireland in the unlikely event of a great British overthrow. This is, that if the existing partnership were to be forcibly dissolved, by external shock, it would mean for Ireland "out of the frying pan into the fire." The idea here is that I have earlier designated as the "bogey man" idea. Germany, or the other victor in the great conflict, would proceed to "take" Ireland. An Ireland administered, say, by Prussians would soon bitterly regret the milder manners of the Anglo-Saxon and pine for the good old days of "doles" from Westminster. I know many Irishmen who admit that as between England and Germany they would prefer to remain in the hands of the former--on the principle that it is better to keep the devil you know than fall into the hands of a new devil.

German rule, you are asked to believe, would be so bad, so stern, that under it Ireland, however much she might have suffered from England in the past, would soon yearn to be restored to the arms of her sorrowing sister. Assuming, for the sake of argument, that Germany "annexed" Ireland, is it at all clear that she would (or even could) injure Ireland more than Great Britain has done? To what purpose and with what end in view? "Innate brutality" – the Englishman replied – "the Prussian always ill-treats those he lays hands on – witness the poor Poles." Without entering into the Polish language question, or the Polish agrarian question, it is permissible for an Irishman to reply that nothing by Prussia in those respects has at all equalled English handling of the Irish language or England land dealings in Ireland. The Polish language still lives in Prussian Poland and much more vigorously than the Irish language survives in Ireland.

But it is not necessary to obscure the issue by reference to the Prussian Polish problem. An Ireland annexed to the German Empire (supposing this to be internationally possible) as one of the fruits of a German victory over Great Britain would clearly be administered as a common possession of the German people, and not as a Prussian province. The analogy, if one can be set up in conditions so dissimilar, would lie not between Prussia and her Polish provinces, but between the German Empire and Alsace-Lorraine. What, then, would be the paramount object of Germany in her administration of an overseas Reichsland of such extraordinary geographical importance to her future as Ireland would be?

Clearly not to impoverish and depress that new-won possession but to enhance its exceeding strategic importance by vigorous and wise administration, so as to make it the main counterpoise to any possible recovery of British maritime supremacy, so largely due as this was in the past to Great Britain's own possession of this island.

A prosperous and flourishing Ireland, recognizing that her own interests lie with those of the new Administration, would assuredly be the first and chief aim of German statesmanship.

The very geographical situation of Ireland would alone ensure wise and able administration by her new rulers had Germany no other and special interest in advancing Irish well-being; for to rule from Hamburg and Berlin a remote island and a discontented people, with a highly discontented and separated

Britain intervening, by methods of exploitation and centralization, would be a task beyond the capacity of German statecraft. German effort, then, would be plainly directed to creating an Ireland satisfied with the change, and fully determined to maintain it.

And it might be remembered that Germany is possibly better equipped, intellectually and educationally, for the task of developing Ireland than even 20th century England. She has already faced a remarkable problem, and largely solved it in her forty years' administration of Alsace-Lorraine. There is a province torn by force from the bleeding side of France and alien in sentiment to her new masters to a degree that Ireland could not be to any changes of authority imposed upon her from without, has, within a short lifetime, doubled in prosperity and greatly increased her population, despite the open arms and insistent call of France, and despite a rule denounced from the first as hateful.

However hateful, the Prussian has proved himself an able administrator and an honest and most capable instructor. In his strong hands Strasburg has expanded from being an ill-kept, pent-in French garrison town to a great and beautiful city. Already a local Parliament gives to the population a sense of autonomy, while the palace and constant presence of an Imperial prince affirms the fact that German Imperialism, far from engrossing and centralizing all the activities and powers of the empire in Berlin, recognizes that German nationality is large enough and great enough to admit of many capitals, many individualities, and many separate State growths within the sure compass of one great organism.

That an Ireland severed by force of arms from the British Empire and annexed to the German Empire would be ill-governed by her new masters is inconceivable. On the contrary, the ablest brains in Germany, scientific, commercial, and financial, no less than military and strategic, would be devoted to the great task of making sure the conquest not only of an island but of the intelligence of a not unintelligent people, and by wisely developing so priceless a possession to reconcile its inhabitants through growing prosperity and an excellent administration, to so great a change in their political environment. Can it be said that England, even in her most lucid intervals, has brought to the Government of Ireland her best efforts, her most capable men, or her highest purpose? The answer may be given by Li Hung Chang, whose diary we have so lately read. Recording his interview with Mr. Gladstone, the Chinese statesman says: "He spoke about ... Ireland; and I was certain that he hoped to see that unhappy country governed better before he died. 'They have given their best to England,' he said, 'and in return have been given only England's worst.'" It is certain that Germany, once in possession of Ireland, would assuredly not give to that country only Germany's worst.

In a score of ways Ireland would stand to gain from the change of direction, of purpose, of intention, and, I will add, of inspiration and capacity in her newly-imposed rulers.

Whether she liked them or not, at the outset, would be beside the question. In this they would differ but little from those she had so long and wearily had measure of, and if they brought to their new task a new spirit and a new intellectual equipment Irishmen would not be slow to realize that if they themselves were never to rule their own country, they had, at least, found in their new masters something more than emigration agents.

Moreover, to Germany there would be no "Irish question," no "haggard and haunting problem" to palsy her brain and miscredit her hand with its old tags and jibes and sordid impulses to deny the obvious.

To Germany there would be only an English question. To prevent that from ever again imperilling her world future would be the first purpose of German overseas statesmanship. And it is clear that a wise and capable Irish Administration, designed to build up and strengthen from within and not to belittle and exploit from without, would be the sure and certain purpose of a victorious Germany.

I have now outlined the two possible dispositions of Ireland that up to this British opinion admits as conceivable in die improbable event of a British defeat by Germany. Only these two contingencies are ever admitted. First that Ireland, sharing the common disaster, must endure with her defeated partner all the evils that a great overthrow must inflict upon the United Kingdom. Second, that Ireland, if Great Britain should be completely defeated, might conceivably be "taken" or annexed by the victor and held as a conquered territory, and in this guise would bitterly regret the days of her union with Great Britain. I have sought to show, in answer to the latter argument, that were annexation by the victor indeed to follow a British defeat Ireland might very conceivably find the changed circumstances greatly to her advantage.

But there is a third contingency I have nowhere seen discussed or hinted at, and yet it is at least as likely as No. 1, and far more probable than No. 2 – for I do not think that the annexation of Ireland by a European power is internationally possible, however decisive might be the overthrow of England. It is admitted (and it is upon this hypothesis that the discussion is proceeding) that Great Britain might be defeated by Germany, and that the British fleet might be broken and an enemy's sword might transfix England. Such an overthrow would be of enormous import to Europe and to the whole world. The trident would have changed hands, for the defeat of England could only be brought about by the destruction of her sea supremacy. Unless help came from without, a blockaded Britain would be more at the mercy of the victor than France was after Sedan and Paris. It would lie with the victor to see that the conditions of peace he imposed were such as, while ensuring to him the objects for which he had fought, would be the least likely conditions to provoke external intervention or a combination of alarmed world interests. Now, putting aside lesser consideration, the chief end Germany would have in a war with England would be to ensure her own free future on the seas. For with that assured and guaranteed by a victory over England, all else that she seeks must in the end be hers. To annex resisting British colonies would be in itself an impossible task, physically a much more impossible task than to annex Ireland.

To annex Ireland would be, as a military measure, once command of the seas was gained, a comparatively easy task. No practical resistance to one German army corps even could be offered by any force Ireland contains, or could of herself, put into the field. No arsenal or means of manufacturing arms exists. The population has been disarmed for a century, and by bitter experience has been driven to regard the use of arms as a criminal offence. Patriotism has been treated as felony. Volunteers and Territorials are not for Ireland. To expect that a disarmed and demoralized population who have been sedulously batoned into a state of physical and moral dejection, should develop military virtues in face of a disciplined army is to attribute to Irishmen the very qualities their critics unite in denying them. "The Irishman fights well everywhere except in Ireland," has passed into a commonplace: and since every effort of government has been directed to ensuring the abiding application of the sneer, Englishmen would find, in the end, the emasculating success of their rule completely justified in the physical submission of Ireland to the new force that held her down. With Great Britain cut off and the Irish Sea held by German squadrons, no power from within could maintain any effective resistance to a German occupation of Dublin and a military administration of the island. To convert that into permanent administration could not be opposed from within, and with Great Britain down and severed from Ireland by a victorious German navy, it is obvious that opposition to the permanent retention of Ireland by the victor must come from without, and it is for this international reason that I think a German annexation of any part of a defeated United Kingdom need not be seriously considered. Such a complete change in the geography of Europe as a German-owned Ireland could not but provoke universal alarm and a widespread combination to forbid its realization. The bogey that Ireland, if not John Bull's other island, must necessarily be somebody else's other island will not really bear inspection at close quarters.

Germany would have to attain her end, the permanent disabling of the maritime supremacy of Great Britain, by another and less provocative measure. It is here and in just these circumstances that the third contingency, and one no Englishman I venture to think, has ever dreamed of, would be born on the field of battle and baptized a Germanic godchild with European diplomacy as sponsor. Germany, for her own imperial ends and in pursuit of a great world policy, might successfully accomplish what Louis XIV and Napoleon only contemplated. An Ireland, already severed by a sea held by German warships, and temporarily occupied by a German army, might well be permanently and irrevocably severed from Great Britain, and with common assent erected into a neutralized, independent European State under international guarantees. An independent Ireland would, of itself, be no threat or hurt to any European interest. On the contrary, to make of Ireland an Atlantic Holland, a maritime Belgium, would be an act of restoration to Europe of this the most naturally favoured of European islands that a Peace Congress should, in the end, be glad to ratify at the instance of a victorious Germany. That Germany should propose this form of dissolution of the United Kingdom in any interests but her own, or for the *beaux yeux* of Ireland I do not for a moment assert. Her main object would be the opening of the seas and their permanent freeing from that overwhelming control Great Britain has exercised since the destruction of the French navy, largely based, as all naval strategists must perceive on the unchallenged possession of Ireland.

That Ireland is primarily a European island inhabited by a European people who are not English, and who have for centuries appealed to Europe and the world to aid them in ceasing to be politically controlled by England, is historic fact. And since the translation of this historic fact into practice European politics would undoubtedly effect the main object of the victorious power, it is evident that, Great Britain once defeated, Germany would carry the Irish question to a European solution in harmony with her maritime interests, and could count on the support of the great bulk of European opinion to support the settlement those interests imposed. And if politically and commercially an independent and neutral Irish State commended itself to Europe, on moral and intellectual grounds the claim could be put still higher. Nothing advanced on behalf of England could meet the case for a free Ireland as stated by Germany. Germany would attain her ends as the champion of national liberty and could destroy England's naval supremacy for all time by an act of irreproachable morality. The United States, however distasteful from one point of view the defeat of England might be, could do nothing to oppose a European decision that could dearly win an instant support from influential circles – Irish and German – within her own borders.

In any case the Monroe Doctrine cuts both ways, and unless at the outset the United States could be drawn into an Anglo-Teutonic conflict, it is clear that the decision of a European Congress to create a new European State out of a very old European people could not furnish ground for American interference.

I need not further labour the question. If Englishmen will but awaken from the dream that Ireland "belongs" to them and not to the Irish people, and that that great and fertile island, inhabited by a brave, a chivalrous and an intellectual race (qualities they have alas! done their utmost to expel from the island) is a piece of real estate they own and can dispose of as they will, they cannot fail to perceive that the Irish question cannot much longer be mishandled with impunity, and that far from being, as they now think it, merely a party question – and not even a "domestic question" or one the colonies have a voice in – it may in a brief epoch become a European question.

With the approaching disappearance of the Near Eastern question (which England is hastening to the detriment of Turkey) a more and more pent-in Central Europe may discover that there is a Near Western question, and that Ireland – a free Ireland – restored to Europe is the key to unlock the western ocean and open the seaways of the world.

Again it is Mr. Gladstone who comes to remind Englishmen that Ireland, after all, is a European island, and that Europe has some distant standing in the issue.

"I would beseech Englishmen to consider how they would behave to Ireland, if instead of having 5,000,000 of people, she had 25,000,000; or if instead of being placed between us and the ocean she were placed between us and the Continent." (Notes and queries on the Irish Demand, February, 1887.) While the geographical positions of the islands to each other and to Europe have not changed, and cannot change, the political relation of one to the other, and so the political and economical relation of both to Europe, to the world and to the carrying trade of the world and the naval policies of the powers may be gravely altered by agencies beyond the control of Great Britain.

The changes wrought in the speed and capacity of steam shipping, the growth and visible trend of German naval power, and the increasing possibilities of aerial navigation, all unite to emphasize the historian Niebuhr's warning, and to indicate for Ireland a possible future of restored communion with Europe, and less and less the continued wrong of that artificial exclusion in which British policy has sought to maintain her – "an island beyond an island."

Chapter IX

The Elsewhere Empire

Every man born in Ireland holds a "hereditary brief" for the opponents of English sway, wherever they may be. The tribunal of history in his own land is closed to him; he must appeal to another court; he must seek the ear of those who make history elsewhere. The Irishman is denied the right of having a history, as he is denied the right of having a country. He must recover both. For him there is no past any more than a future. And if he seeks the record of his race in the only schools or books open to him he will find that hope has been shut out of the school and fame taken out of the story.

The late John Richard Green, one of the greatest of English historians, was attracted to Ireland by a noble sympathy for the fallen which he shared with very few of his fellow-countrymen. We are told that he sympathized with the spirit of Irish nationality. "A State," he would say, "is accidental; it can be made or unmade; but a nation is something real which can be neither made nor destroyed."

He had once planned a history of Ireland, "but abandoned the idea because the continuous record of misery and misgovernment was too painful to contemplate." All pleasure lies in contrast. The history of Ireland offers no contrast; it is a tale of unmitigated wrong.

It is too full of graves and the ghosts are not laid yet. As well write the history of a churchyard. Forty years before John Richard Green thus explained why he had abandoned the plan of the graveyard, Victor Hugo lashed the front of England with this very thong. "Ireland turned into a cemetery; Poland transported to Siberia; all Italy a galleys – there is where we stand in this month of November, 1831!"

The history of Ireland remains to be written, because the purpose of Ireland remains yet to be achieved. The widow of John Richard Green has laid the foundations of that temple of hope in which the youth of Ireland must enter and be sworn to the task that yet remains for Irishmen to accomplish.

And so in closing the days of 1913 I bring, with a message of hope, these scattered thoughts upon the British Empire and its approaching dissolution to lay before the youth of Ireland. I say approaching dissolution advisedly, for the signs are there to be read. "Home Rule" will not save it. The attempt now being made to bribe Ireland and the greater Ireland beyond the seas, to the side of the Elsewhere Empire by what has been aptly termed a "ticket-of-leave" bill, will not suffice. The issue lies in stronger hands. Even could the two Irelands be won by the dole now offered, of a subordinate Parliament in Dublin, its hands tied so that it must be impotent for any national effort, "a Parliament" as Mr. Herbert Samuel says, "for the local affairs of Irishmen," there are other and more powerful agencies that no measure of conciliation within the Empire can permanently win to that system of world exploitation centred in London.

"I would let the Irish have Home Rule," said recently Mr. Winston Churchill, "for their own idiotic affairs." But the last word came from Lord Morley, the "father of Home Rule." "Give it them," he said, in friendly, private counsel, "give it them; let them have the full savour of their own dunghill civilization."

But the last word of all will come, not from Lord Morley, or "Home Rule," but from the land and the myriad peoples whose ancient civilization, Lord Morley, like every preceding Viceroy, has striven to bury under the dunghill of British supremacy in India, and to hide the very outlines of the ancient body of the set designs of a new purpose. The capital of British India is to be the "new Delhi," planned in Whitehall, but paid for in India – the apotheosis of dung. The new India will make short work of "the new Delhi."

"An unplumbed, salt, estranging sea" of moral and spiritual separation sets between the imperial conception as nourished in Britain and the growing hope of the great millions of mankind who make up the greatest realm of her empire.

Ireland *might* be bought or bribed, at any rate in this generation, to forfeit her national ideals and barter the aspiration that six centuries of contact with England have failed to kill; but the 350,000,000 of Indian mankind can never be, or bought, or bribed in the end.

Even if Ireland forgot the deathless words of Grattan, delivered in the subordinate Parliament of 1780, those words will find a response in the hearts of men who never heard of Grattan. For the voice of the Irish patriot was, in truth, a world voice – a summons to every audience wherever men gather in quest of freedom. The prophesy Grattan uttered in the name of Ireland assuredly will be fulfilled, and that in the life time of many of us, in that greater Ireland England holds in the eastern seas by the very same tide of raid, conquest and spoliation that has given her our own land.

Substitute India for Ireland and the Grattan of 1780 becomes the Indian patriot of to-day.

> "I will never be satisfied so long as the meanest cottager in Ireland has a link of the British chain clanking in his rags; he may be naked, he shall not be in irons; and I do see the time is at hand; the spirit has gone forth, the declaration is planted; and though great men should apostasize, yet the cause will live; and though the public speaker should die, yet the immortal fire shall outlast the organ which conveyed it, and the breath of liberty, like the word of holy men, will not die with the prophet, but survive him."

Were Ireland to accept the bribe now offered she would indeed justify the reproach of Wilfred Blunt; but she would become some thing else than a "weapon of offence in England's hands against the freedom of the world elsewhere;" she would share, and rightly share the fate of the parasite growth that, having gripped her trunk so tightly, has by that aid reached the sunlight. The British Empire is no northern oak tree. It is a creeping, climbing plant that has fastened on the limbs of others and grown great from a sap not its own. If we seek an analogy for it in the vegetable and not in the animal world we must go to the forests of the tropics and not to the northland woodlands. In the great swamps at the mouth of the Amazon the naturalist Bates describes a monstrous liana, the "Sipo Matador" or Murdering Creeper, that far more fitly than the oak tree of the north typifies John Bull and the place he has won in the sunlight by the once strong limbs of Ireland.

Speaking of the forests round Para, Bates says: – "In these tropical forests each plant and tree seems to be striving to outvie its fellows, struggling upwards towards light and air – branch and leaf and stem – regardless of its neighbours. Parasitic plants are seen fastening with firm grip on others, making use of them with reckless indifference as instruments for their own advancement. Live and let live is clearly not the maxim taught in these wildernesses. There is one kind of parasitic tree very common near Para which exhibits this feature in a very prominent manner. It is called the "Sipo Matador," or Murderer Liana. It belongs to the fig order, and has been described and figured by Von Martius as the Atlas to Spix and Martius' Travels. I observed many specimens. *The base of its stem would be unable to bear the weight of the upper growth*; it is obliged therefore to support itself on a tree of *another species*. In this it is not essentially different from other climbing trees and plants, but the way the Matador sets about it is peculiar and produces certainly a disagreeable impression. It springs up close to the tree on which it intends to fix itself, and the wood of its stem grows by spreading itself like a plastic mould over one side of the trunk of its supporter. It then puts forth, from each side, an armlike branch, which grows rapidly, and looks as though a stream of sap were flowing and hardening as it went. This adheres closely to the trunk of the victim, and the two arms meet at the opposite side and blend together. These arms are put forth at somewhat regular intervals in mounting upwards, and the victim, when its strangler is full grown, becomes tightly clasped by a number of inflexible rings. These rings gradually grow larger as the Murderer flourishes, rearing its crown of foliage to the sky mingled with that of its neighbour, and in course of time they kill it, by stopping the flow of its sap.

The strange spectacle now remains of the selfish parasite clasping in its arms the lifeless and decaying body of its victim, which had been a help to its own growth. Its ends have been served – it has flowered and fruited, reproduced and disseminated its kind; and *now when the dead trunk moulders away its own end approaches; its support is gone and itself also falls.*"

The analogy is almost the most perfect in literature, and if we would not see it made perfect in history we must get rid of the parasite grip before we are quite strangled. If we would not share the coming darkness we must shake off the murderer's hold, before murderer and victim fall together. That fall is close at hand. A brave hand may yet cut the "Sipo Matador," and the slayer be slain before he has quite stifled his victim.

If that hand be not a European one, then may it come, bronzed, keen, and supple from the tropic calm! The birds of the forest are on the wing.

Regions Caesar never knew, including Hibernia, have come under the eagles, nay the vultures, of imperial Britain. But the lion's maw is full.

At length the overgorged beast of prey, with all the diseases in his veins that over-eating brings, finds that his claws are not so sharp as they were, that his belly is much heavier when he tries to leap and that it is now chiefly by his voice he still scares his enemies.

The Empire of England dates from Tudor times. Henry VIII was the first John Bull. When the conquered Irish and the wealth derived from their rich country England set out to lay low every free people that had a country worth invading and who, by reasons of their non-imperial instinct were not prepared to meet her on equal terms. India she overran by the same methods as had given her Ireland.

Wholesale plunder, treachery and deceit met at her council board under a succession of Governors and Viceroys, whose policy was that of Captain Kidd, and whose ante-room of state led every native prince to the slippery plank. The thing became the most colossal success upon earth. No people were found able to withstand such a combination. How could peoples still nursed in the belief of some diviner will ruling men's minds resist such an attack?

For one brief space Napoleon reared his head; and had he cast his vision to Ireland instead of to Egypt he would have found out the secret of the pirate's stronghold. But the fates willed otherwise; the time was not yet. He sailed for Alexandria, lured by a dream, instead of for Cork; and the older Imperialists beat the new Imperialists and secured a fresh century of unprecedented triumph. The Pyramids looked down on Waterloo; but the headlands of Bantry Bay concealed the mastery, and the mystery, of the seas.

With 1811 was born the era of Charles Peace, no less than of John Bull on Sundays and Saint's days a churchwarden, who carried the plate; on week days a burglar who lifted it. Truly, as John Mitchel said on his convict hulk: "On English felony the sun never sets." May it set in 1915.

From Napoleon's downfall to the battle of Colenso, the Empire founded by Henry VIII has swelled to monstrous size. Innumerable free peoples have bit the dust and died with plaintive cries to heaven. The wealth of London has increased a thousand fold, and the giant hotels and caravanserais have grown, at the millionaire's touch, to rival the palaces of the Caesars.

"All's well with God's world" – and poet and plagiarist, courtier and courtesan, Kipling and cant--these now dally by the banks of the Thames and dine off the peoples of the earth, just as once the degenerate populace of imperial Rome fed upon the peoples of the Pyramids. But the thing is near the end. The "secret of Empire" is no longer the sole possession of England. Other peoples are learning to think imperially. The Goths and the Visigoths of modern civilisation are upon the horizon. Action must soon follow thought. London, like Rome, will have strange guests. They will not pay their hotel bills. Their day is not yet but it is at hand. "Home Rule" assemblies and Indian "Legislative Councils" may prolong the darkness; but the dawn is in die sky. And in the downfall of the Tudor Empire, both Ireland and India shall escape from the destruction and join again the free civilizations of the earth.

The birds of the forest are on the wing.

It is an Empire in these straights that turns to America, through Ireland, to save it. And the price it offers is--war with Germany. France may serve for a time, but France like Germany, is in Europe, and in the end it is all Europe and not only Germany England assails. Permanent confinement of the white races, as distinct from the Anglo-Saxon variety, can only be achieved by the active support and close alliance of the American people. These people are to-day, unhappily republicans and free men, and have no ill-will for Germany and a positive distaste for imperialism. It is not really in their blood. That blood is mainly Irish and German, the blood of men not distinguished in the past for successful piracy and addicted rather to the ways of peace. The wars that Germany has waged have been wars of defence, or wars to accomplish the unity of her people. Irish wars have been only against one enemy, and ending always in material disaster they have conferred always a moral gain. Their memory uplifts the Irish heart; for no nation, no people, can reproach Ireland with having wronged them. She has injured no man.

And now, to-day, it is the great free race of this common origin of peace-loving peoples, filling another continent, that is being appealed to by every agency of crafty diplomacy, in every garb but that of truth, to aid the enemy of both and the arch-disturber of the old world. The jailer of Ireland seeks Irish-American support to keep Ireland in prison; the intriguer against Germany would win German-American good-will against its parent stock. There can be no peace for mankind, no limit to the intrigues set on foot to assure Great Britain "the mastery of the seas."

If "America" will but see things aright, as a good "Anglo-Saxon" people should, she will take her place beside, nay, even a little in front of John Bull in the plunder of the earth. Were the "Anglo-Saxon Alliance" ever consummated it would be the biggest crime in human history. That alliance is meant by the chief party seeking it to be a perpetual threat to the peoples of Europe, nay, to the whole of mankind outside the allied ranks. And instead of bringing peace it must assuredly bring the most distracting and disastrous conflict that has ever stained the world with blood.

John Bull has now become the great variety artist, one in truth whose infinite variety detention cannot stale any more than Customs officers can arrest the artist's baggage.

At one moment the "Shirt King," being prosecuted for the sale of cheap cottons as "Irish Linen" in London; the next he lands the "Bloater King" in New York, offering small fish as something very like a whale. And the offer in both cases is made in the tongue of Shakespeare.

The tongue has infinite uses; from China it sounds the "call for prayer," and lo, the Book of Dividends opens at the right text. Were Bull ever caught in the act, and put from the trade of international opium-dosing to that of picking oakum and the treadmill we should hear him exclaim, as he went out of sight, "Behold me weaving the threads of democratic destiny as I climb the golden stair."

The rôles are endless! In Ireland, the conversion of Irishmen into cattle; in England, the conversion of Irish cattle into men; in India and Egypt the suppression of the native press; in America the subsidising of the non-native press; the tongue of Shakespeare has infinite uses. He only poached deer – it would poach dreadnoughts. The emanations of Thames sewage are all over the world, and the sewers are running still. The penalty for the pollution of the Thames is a high one; but the prize for the pollution of the Mississippi is still higher; the fountains of the deep, the mastery of the great waters, these are the things John Bull seeks on the shore of the "Father of Waters."

The sunset of the fading Empire would turn those waters into blood. The British Empire was not founded in peace; how, then can it be kept by peace, or ensured by peace-treaties? It was born of pillage and blood-shed, and has been maintained by both; and it cannot now be secured by a common language any more than a common Bible. The lands called the British Empire belong to many races, and it is only by the sword and not by the Book of Peace or any pact of peace that those races can be kept from the ownership of their own countries.

The "Anglo-Saxon Alliance" means a compact to ensure slavery and beget war. The people who fought the greatest war in modern history to release slaves are not likely to begin the greatest war in all history to beget slaves.
Let the truth be known in America that England wants to turn the great Republic of free men into die imperial ally of the great Empire of bought men, and that day die "Anglo-Saxon Alliance" gives place to the Declaration of Independence.

The true alliance to aim at for all who love peace is the friendly Union of Germany, America and Ireland. These are the true United States of the world.

Ireland, the link between Europe and America, must be freed by both.

Denied to-day free intercourse with either, she yet forms in the great designs of Providence the natural bond to bring the old world and the new together.

May 1915 lay the foundation of this – the true Hundred Years of Peace!